Women Finishing Well

Building a Legacy of Faith
That Lasts for Generations

Chris Syme

CONTENTS

INTRODUCTION

Therefore, since we are surrounded by such a great cloud of witnesses, let us throw off everything that hinders and the sin that so easily entangles. And let us run with perseverance the race marked out for us.

– Hebrews 12:1

In my days as a college sports event manager, outdoor track and field meets were my favorite. There was so much to see. The running events usually culminate with the 4x100 meter relays. In this four-hundred-meter race a team consisting of four sprinters runs one hundred meters each in a flurry of baton passes to get that metal cylinder across the finish line. The goal is not to get the last runner across the finish line but to get the baton across the finish line. If the baton is dropped or not passed in the "exchange zone," the team is disqualified. It is a magnificent display of synchrony at high speeds.

Seeing the 4x100 meter relay play out is a perfect picture of what it means to finish well. You are carrying a baton of faith. It consists of your legacy; all your life stories with all the people God has put in your life. Jesus has called us *all* to go through life influencing people for him (Mt. 28:19-20). And you already have a circle of influence—people God has surrounded you with—as your starting block.

Who are you passing the baton to? For some of you, it may be your family: your children, your grandchildren, your extended family. For others, it may be people at work. It may be your church family, your neighbors, or your book club. There is no pre-defined circle of influence for everyone. There is only a baton in your hand to pass.

All women share some unique opportunities and struggle with some common concerns. Many younger women are pursuing a full life of family and career. But some are finding their lives so full that when it comes to serving at a church or in a ministry, they're lucky to just show up. As Baby Boomers and beyond, we're thinking about leaving careers and empty nests to serve God in our second wind. But many of us are finding that our gifts and talents are irrelevant to a church desperately trying to reach the younger generations. This study is about rekindling our passion for serving God, and refocusing energies on the people God has put right in front of us—those we are surrounded with. In some seasons, that means serving in a church or ministry or nonprofit. In other seasons that means caregiving a spouse, or taking care of young children at home. But whatever season we're in, we are building a legacy that will last for generations.

Running the Marathon

Life is actually more like a marathon than a four-hundred-meter relay race. Life happens. We may find ourselves running a different race than the one we started, or not running at all. Maybe we stopped for a water break, got distracted and dropped the baton, or just couldn't make it up that last hill. We wanted to finish well but now we just hope to finish, period.

Under Armor pro marathoner Nick Arciniaga runs marathons for a living. Can you imagine a more challenging job? I can't. He recommends a four-part plan to train for a marathon. And with a little poetic license, we can use the same plan to help us run the race marked out for us:

1. *Manage your energy.* The first part of the race is a warm-up. Remember those early years of life? All the exuberance, all the plans? Always keep running with the end goal in mind. Don't expend all your energy too early. It's a long haul.
2. *Create an effective, flexible plan.* The storms of changing weather demand flexibility when running a marathon. In one 26.2-mile stretch you can experience pouring rain to bright sunshine to snow. Always know where your peace is anchored and be ready for any onslaught that comes your way.

3. *Break the race up into segments*. Arciniaga says our minds are more willing to tackle one segment at a time because each part of the race has its own unique challenges. Surveying the whole race at once can be daunting. Embrace your season.
4. *Choose to race with confidence*. Confidence creates fortitude. Know the course, know your Guide, know your purpose.[1]

My Marathon

This book is the result of 16 years of procrastination—something that makes me wince as I write it. When I finished graduate school in 2002, I had an encounter with God that convinced me He had a specific purpose for me to follow. It was so real I couldn't get away from it. But I tried. Hard.

I made the first step by getting a two-year certificate in Pastoral Leadership. But leadership opportunities didn't go along with the certificate. So I turned back to my graduate degree and pursued my passion for teaching at a university, and then as a media relations professional in college athletics. I continued to be involved in church; all the while feeling something tugging at my sleeve. I just kept shaking it off. I went through the morning devotions motions, but I'm not sure I really wanted to hear from God. I was afraid of what He might want me to do. Life was good, for the most part.

I continued to climb the ladder I had put up against the wrong building. Then I made a decision that started the gears of change turning; I decided to host a small women's Bible study. We were studying a book about finding our purpose—I can't even remember the name. All I know is that a deep-seeded disappointment that I wasn't going to finish well on my present course started to nag me. Then in 2011 my mother passed away after a long and painful struggle with dementia. I had already quit my job the year before to help my Dad care for her while establishing a consulting practice.

---

[1] Nick Arciniaga, "4 Strategies from a Pro to Run Your Best Marathon," mapmyrun blog, November 30, 2015, https://blog.mapmyrun.com/4-strategies-from-a-pro-to-run-your-best-marathon/.

Discussions about finishing well started to pop up in our little Bible study. All women of the same vintage, we started sharing our sentiments of not feeling our lives were making a difference. I started desperately looking for Bible studies inspiring women to finish well. There really weren't any. So after four years of more procrastination, I sat down and started an outline. I didn't think it would go anywhere. I really felt that God wanted me to write this study for myself to regain my passion for serving the people God already had in my life. My life's focus began to shift. That nagging feeling tugging on my sleeve had made its way into my heart and I was determined.

I started sharing my journey with women in the lobby at church, sitting around the table at Starbucks, in my own living room, and just about anywhere that anyone would listen. I soon realized I wasn't the only one that felt this way. Women asked if they could see the book after I was finished and I was a little embarrassed. I wasn't sure it was for anyone's eyes but mine. But my closest friend encouraged me to start a podcast and agreed to help. By this time, I was deep into a process of weaving God into my everyday that I knew was responsible for my evolution. I call it First Things First and you'll see it throughout this book. God gave me a desire to share my journey with other women, so I humbly pass it on to you.

Embrace the Challenge

It is my heart's desire to help you finish well. I want to see you build a legacy of faith that will bless the people God has put in your life now and for generations to come. I pray you would be confident that you can be an influence for God no matter where you are in life: as a grandmother or a caregiver, alone or surrounded by family, in a mission field or in your living room, in the workplace or in your community. Finishing well is a life lived on purpose. May you discover yours here.

Getting Started with This Study

This journey to finish well is divided into three parts:

- The Spiritual Foundation: The understructure for building a legacy life that lasts is the first and most important step.
- Training for the Race: Whatever path we are building needs tools, habits, practice and perseverance.
- Your Personal Legacy Plan: Putting it all together, building your custom journey, picking up your baton, and getting to the starting line.

Your Journey Needs a Road Map

Before you get started, you will need a notebook or journal to chronicle your journey. You'll want to make note of verses that pull at your heart and ideas or concepts you want to remember. Where is God challenging you? Write it down. Believe me, you'll come back to your journal in awe of how God is leading you. If you've never kept a journal before, it will be a beautiful adventure.

Each chapter is followed by three study sessions. Pray that God will open the eyes of heart as you dig in and apply what you've read. Don't hurry through. Take time to listen and reflect.

Who Needs This Study

This study is for women at every possible station of life. Leaving a legacy is not attached to a specific age or lifestyle, and it doesn't matter if you are wheelchair bound or running marathons. It doesn't matter if you are a mother with children still in your home, working full-time, or not working at all. You may be a caregiver for a loved one, a widow, a single unmarried woman, or a grandmother of twenty. Together we make a beautiful mosaic of blessing for the next generations.

Warning: This Book Can Change Your Life

With any change comes some discomfort. But that's not a bad thing. The longer you drive along in that muddy rut of routine, the deeper it gets and the harder it is to get out. But that sludge is deceptive—it looks like the only way through. But it's not. It's just the same old path to the same old destination. It's comfortable—until the ruts get so deep, we get stuck. Then we spin our wheels a while and decide maybe that's as far as we can go. *Don't settle for the rut.* Driving out can be hard work. And I've said that from experience in the rut. But God's got you, and I am here to cheer you on.

I am praying for you—praying that you will rise up with a new passion and join women everywhere who want to influence the people God brings into their lives. I wish I could be sitting with you at your kitchen counter with a cup of coffee or hot tea, praying with you and encouraging you to keep running the race. Know that I am with you in spirit.

The righteous will flourish like a palm tree, they will grow like a cedar of Lebanon; planted in this house of the LORD, they will flourish in the courts of our God. They will still bear fruit in old age, they will stay fresh and green, proclaiming, "The LORD is upright; he is my Rock, and there is no wickedness in Him. (Psalm 92:12-15)

PART ONE

BUILDING A LIFE LEGACY
THAT LASTS FOR GENERATIONS

"We all must either wear out or rust out, every one of us. My choice is to wear out."

—Theodore Roosevelt

"Therefore, since we are surrounded by such a great cloud of witnesses, let us throw off everything that hinders and the sin that so easily entangles, and let us run with perseverance the race marked out for us."

—Hebrews 12:1

What We Leave Behind

After my mother-in-law's funeral, my husband and his siblings began the arduous task of sorting through a lifetime of family possessions. Like many people married during the Depression era, his parents had a basement full of memories that dated back to their early marriage years. Sorting through what to keep would be a chore. But she had made some decisions ahead. Years before she passed away, she had asked her grandchildren to choose some items they wanted for themselves after she was gone.

As I surveyed the items the grandkids had requested, a pattern emerged: they were looking for pieces of experiential memories—things that made them think of personal time spent with Grandma not something that would gather dust on a bedroom shelf. One wanted a small metal spatula—something that the grown-ups would have tossed in the Salvation Army pile but something that sparked a granddaughter's memories of baking and frosting chocolate sheet cake bars together. Another wanted her sewing machine, certainly not new or fancy by today's standards but that didn't matter. She just wanted something that would evoke fond memories of cotton cloth laid out on the dining room table, pinning on tissue paper patterns, and scissors flying in Grandma's hands.

This woman they had come to know as Grandma had read them books, taught them to crochet, knit, bake, sew, garden, churn homemade ice cream, and dance the two-step. She had opened her home to any relatives passing through and graciously fed them all whatever was in the freezer. She had passed on a legacy they all wanted to not just remember but carry on.

What builds and strengthens a lasting legacy is experiential connection. In these first chapters we'll look at how God builds that connection with His people through love and grace.

When we think of a legacy we may think of a trust, a collection of material assets to be passed along after we die. Or we may even think of a legacy as a collection of stories we hope people will remember. But a legacy isn't just about knickknacks or savings bonds or albums full of old pictures. A legacy is about *investing* your life into the lives of those God has placed around you. That *infusion of purpose* inspires generations after you to build their own legacy. And that is the kind of legacy that lasts for generations.

The Firm Foundation

Part one of the study is about building the biblical definition of a legacy life—what the Bible says about finishing well. We'll be backing up the beeping cement truck to pour the foundation of God's principles about how to build a life that can influence generations to come.

And speaking of influence, we'll also define your circle of influence and your communities of influence: the potential recipients of your legacy life. And it's more than just family. There is no one mold or template that applies to who you are influencing. We are not all grandmothers. Some of us are disconnected from our families by distance or dissonance. We are not all married. Some of us are widowed, some are divorced, and some have never married. Some of us still work full time. Some of us have never worked outside our homes. Some of us are contemplating retirement right now. Some of us lead active lives in our communities, and some of us are homebodies. No matter where we are in life, we are influencing people for God (Matt. 5:16).

My mother-in-law wasn't a highly educated woman. She never had a career outside the home. She lived seven miles from the nearest town that boasted only two grocery stores, four churches, and six taverns. Her legacy wasn't lots of money or a pile of stocks and bonds but a life spent serving others and loving God. She possessed a true north that pointed to what was important in life. She was running the race marked out for her, and she finished well. She left a legacy that is already influencing generations beyond her.

CHAPTER ONE

RUNNING TO PASS THE BATON

GOD'S LEGACY BLUEPRINT

Do you see what this means—all these pioneers who blazed the
way, all these veterans cheering us on? It means we'd better get on
with it. Strip down, start running—and never quit! No extra
spiritual fat, no parasitic sins. Keep your eyes on *Jesus*, who both
began and finished this race we're in.

—Hebrews 12: 1-3, The Message

So don't sit around on your hands! No more dragging your feet!
Clear the path for long-distance runners so no one will trip and fall,
so no one will step in a hole and sprain an ankle. Help each other
out. And run for it!

—Hebrews 12:12-13, The Message

What Is A Legacy of Faith?

The *Merriam-Webster Dictionary* defines a legacy as, "something
transmitted by or received from an ancestor or predecessor or from
the past." A legacy is a gift we pass on. For better or for worse, it is
our gift to those God places in our lives.

The Bible's definition of legacy is a life lived out loving God and
loving people. It is an intricate portrait of people, places, and events
that the Master Artist creates for each one of us—a mosaic of
experiences that is passed on and has the power to bless many
generations.

Hebrews 12 opens with an image of each of us surrounded by a huge crowd of witnesses (v.1). If we close our eyes, we can see the faces of those people who impacted our life and passed their baton of faith to us. Some of them we remember and some of them we have only read about. Their stories inspire us. Because of their journey, we are encouraged to strip off every weight that hinders us and run the race set before us. That race takes endurance and self-discipline (vv. 2-11). And sometimes the race feels like we're running a marathon—uphill.

At the end of Hebrews 12, the author speaks of those running the race behind us (12-13). We are making a level path for them so they can run swiftly on even terrain. These long-distance runners are the people we are building a legacy for. It's up to us to clear a path for them and pass our baton.

A Tale of Two Legacies

In Exodus 20, we see the Old Testament version of legacy as God gives Moses the ten commandments for the Jewish nation. What a magnificent and terrible day that must have been for the nation of Israel. God was about to change their lives forever. After two days of intense preparation, the third day began with thunder, lightning, and a blasting of trumpets that made the whole community tremble. Talk about a grand entrance. As Moses led the cowering community out to meet God, the trumpets grew louder, and a thick, dark cloud of smoke covered the trembling mountain. God had their attention.

The second commandment God gave Moses is a conditional promise for the nation of Israel (Ex. 20:4-6). In it, God outlines two legacies from which they could choose: one of continuing trouble and one of continuing love. The first path God reveals is for idolaters, or more specifically for "those who hate [Him]" (v. 5). It's explicit and unambiguous. The word *hate* may seem harsh, but it removes the gray area that the newly liberated nation was famous for—sometimes with God, sometimes not.

Those who hated God were simply defined as those who lived their lives apart from God. They wanted to be in control; they drove the bus and had their own agenda. If they had their way, they would have turned back to Egypt before crossing the Red Sea. To those who hated God, the legacy would be punishing the children for the sin of the parents to the third and fourth generation. No wiggle room there. Hating God brought a legacy of trouble.

The second path is a stark contrast. God said he would show "love to a thousand generations of those who love me and keep my commandments" (Ex. 20:6). No gray area there either. Loving God promised a multigenerational covering of God's love; a legacy of blessing.

What a difference between the two. Both legacies have concrete expectations and consequences. But one will ruin lives until it is stopped, and the other can continually bless many generations as it is carried forward. God, in His infinite mercy, gave Israel a choice.

Time to Pick Up Your Baton

The first step in this journey is making that choice to pick up your baton and get on the starting line. But just how do we reach inside and turn on the switch that leads to action?

As Joshua was getting ready to pass on his baton at the end of his leadership term, he gathered Israel together to renew the covenant God had made with them through Moses. In Joshua 23-24 we see his farewell address. In 24:14-15, he throws down this challenge:

> "Now fear the LORD and serve him with all faithfulness. Throw away the gods your ancestors worshiped beyond the Euphrates River and in Egypt, and serve the LORD. But if serving the LORD seems undesirable to you, then choose for yourselves this day whom you will serve, whether the gods your ancestors served beyond the Euphrates, or the gods of the Amorites, in whose land you are living. But as for me and my household, we will serve the LORD."

Friend, that is your challenge as we start this journey together: the first order of business is making sure our hearts are on the right track.

The Race is Not Over

Believe me, I feel the pain in your hesitation. Some of the frustration we feel comes when we are tempted to believe that the race marked out for us is actually over, and we're just coasting to the finish line. Society tells us we've raised our children, enjoyed our careers, and now it is time to relax. Sure, it's tempting to put our feet up, turn on the TV, or open a good book and just drift away. Maybe we just want to slow down. Or maybe we feel our culture has labeled us irrelevant. Either way, we need a new determination. Our race is not over.

Several years ago I wanted to take up running. My youngest daughter was running half marathons, and I thought it would be fun if we ran one together. I wasn't delusional so I asked her if she would settle for a 5K instead—that's three miles as opposed to thirteen. She agreed, and I began my training.

This 5K wasn't just any race, by the way. It was inside Disneyland. Many of you many not feel giddy about Disneyland, but this was a monster dream for me. I trained like a ninja, all the time visualizing myself running across the finish line with arms held high to be greeted by Mickey and Minnie. Halfway into my twelve-week training I developed a stress fracture in my lower left leg. I was devastated. I had to wear a boot for the next four weeks. My dream of being an elite 5K runner vaporized.

Just about the time my pity party reached its crescendo, I heard my mother's voice in my head. At this time in my life she was lost in full-blown dementia, but her voice was always crystal clear in my head when I needed it. She used to say, "you can't control what life throws at you, but you can control the fight." I couldn't let that voice down. So, I decided to become an elite 5K walker instead. The doctor okayed my plan of trying to walk the course provided my X-ray showed healing, and I promised to stop occasionally to get a picture taken with one of the many Disney characters that line the course and cheer for the runners. My daughter and I finished the walk, arms held high at the finish line. We got a medal and a banana for our efforts, and a hug from Chip and Dale. It was magical.

You might be tempted to quit. One of Satan's biggest lies is that youth equals value. He wants us to think that the older we get, the more invisible we are. Our churches don't know what to do with us; our culture thinks we are a burden. Those lies are part of a big cock-and-bull story the enemy is weaving to keep the largest spiritual army on the face of the earth disheartened and discouraged. It's time to smash that piece of fiction with the truth. God has given us a baton and marked a race out for us. We have generations to influence. Time to get running! Don't give up; don't ever give up.

The apostle Paul, who seemed to do some of his best writing when faced with obstacles, encouraged us to keep pushing ahead regardless of personal circumstances: "Brothers and sisters, I do not consider myself yet to have taken hold of it. But one thing I do: Forgetting what is behind and straining toward what is ahead, I press on toward the goal to win the prize for which God has called me heavenward in Christ Jesus" (Phil. 3:13-14). Paul wasn't done—even sitting in a dark, cramped hole in prison. He wasn't interested in rusting out; he was committed to wearing out. He ran across the finish line with arms held high.

My prayer for you: God, help us to choose this day to do life Your way. Teach us to build a legacy of faith that we can pass on to those precious people You put in our lives. Help us to listen and hold fast to You.

DAY ONE: DIGGING DEEPER

Ask God for wisdom as you consider what stood out to you in this week's reading. Write your thoughts in your study journal. Look intently into God's Word, and you will be blessed in what you do (James 1:25).

1. What is your idea of finishing well and leaving a legacy of faith?
2. Read Deuteronomy 30:19-20. What does it look like for you to "choose life, so that you and your children may live and that you may love the LORD your God, listen to his voice, and hold fast to him"?
3. Read Hebrews 12:12-13. What do you think it might look like in your life to "make level paths for your feet" so that those coming behind you will have a smooth path?
4. Read Joshua 24:14-15. If we look at our life and culture today, what kinds of "other gods" might we be serving that we need to throw away?
5. Make a list of things in your life that might be holding you back from finishing well. These may be things you cannot change as well as things you can. As we go through the study, we will revisit this list.
6. Think of a hard choice that you have had to make in your adult Christian life. Describe the process of seeking God for help and how that influenced your decision one way or another.

DAY TWO: LEGACY BUILDING BLOCKS
DEFINING YOUR CIRCLE OF INFLUENCE

In the introduction introduction to part one we introduced the phrase "circle of influence." Your circle of influence consists of people you interact with regularly and share a deeper level of intimacy with beyond just friendship.

If you look at Jesus' friendship groups in the Bible, you would recognize his inner circle (Peter, James, and John), his disciples (the 12 guys he chose to do life with and equipped to establish the church), and his large group of followers. Your circle of influence is that middle group—not quite as intimate as your inner circle, but characterized by purposeful interaction with a deeper goal than ordinary friendship.

They may be family members, friends, work colleagues, Bible study buddies, or neighbors. They could be differing ages, but they are people you encourage, pray for, and spend purposeful time with.

Truth fact: A woman finishing well builds a circle of influence by creating deep relationships through sharing her life with those close to her.

1. Read James 1:5 and ask for God's promised wisdom to help you identify people in your circle of influence. Be confident in people God sends your way, and don't be surprised if this group changes from time to time.
2. In your journal, make a list of people God brings to your mind. If you're an introvert or struggling to come up with ten or so, ask God to keep the eyes of your heart open for people He may want to bring into your circle of influence.
3. Ask God to show you how you can be an influence for Him in the lives on this list. Add names as people move into your circles of influence.
4. Set aside time tomorrow to pray for the people on your Circle of Influence list. Remember, the length of your prayer is not the key. Praying more often is a better habit to get into. Just reading through the list regularly helps keep them on your mind. God knows who they are.

DAY THREE: FIRST THINGS FIRST
WHY MORNING IS IMPORTANT

Something special happens in the morning right after you lift your eyelids. Your foggy brain starts to wake up to the realization that there is a new day ahead, a brand-new slate, a blank canvas. For some of us, that realization is only a brief moment before thoughts of the day's agenda start pushing and shoving each other for a place in the long line that will form the day.

Throughout the Scriptures we see Jesus and others interacting with God first in their day. Why? Because setting your agenda for the day with God's priorities first will help you see your day through a new pair of glasses, with eternal vision. Before we start our to-do list, we should set our hearts and minds on things above (Col. 3:1-2).

1. Read the following verses. What is the significance of morning in each of these verses?
- Genesis 22:3
- Exodus 8:20
- 1 Samuel 17:20
- Psalm 5:3
- Mark 1:35

First Things First is a commitment to do five short routines every morning—first thing. Each routine starts with the letter *W*. With a short learning curve, they can occupy as few as ten minutes of your day—total. Each *W* is totally customizable to you. I'll give you lots of ideas and tips throughout the study. We'll cover some in part one and some in part two.

The five routines include:

- **W**ake-up call – Dedicate your day to God.
- **W**ater – Drink at least eight good gulps (before coffee, tea, or sugar).
- **W**ord – Spend time interacting with God's Word.
- **W**ait on God with prayer and listening.
- **W**orship – Cultivate the power of personal worship.
1. Put a check mark next those habits above that you already have incorporated into your morning. Underline those you need to work on.

CHAPTER TWO

THE LOVE-OBEDIENCE CONNECTION
WHAT'S LOVE GOT TO DO WITH IT?

If you keep my commands, you will remain in my love, just as I
have kept my Father's commands and remain in his love.

—John 15:10

And this is love: that we walk in obedience to His commands. As
you have heard from the beginning, His command is that you walk
in love.

—2 John:6

A Detour Through the Wilderness

In Exodus 13, the Israelites left Egypt after four hundred years of
being steeped in the Egyptian culture. As the Jews were shaking
the dust out of their bedrolls and getting ready to set out, they
thought they only had about a month of travel ahead. Easy, peasy,
right? But God made a last second change in their itinerary.

It had been a long season of worshipping the same lifeless stone
statues as the Egyptians. God knew they were weak-hearted and
would cut and run back to Egypt at the first sign of trouble (Ex.
13:17-18). It was going to take some time to erase the deep-seated
traditions of their captors, the pungent aromas of Egyptian food,
and the comfortable roofs over their heads. And, oh yeah, the
slavery. God also knew they were going to suffer some convenient
memory loss when the going got tough. It was going to be a long
and winding road of testing their obedience.

God took them through the wilderness to refine them not to punish them. He wanted their full allegiance and attention once they arrived at their destination. He wanted them to be prepared for the promised land life, so they would be successful in the ensuing battles they would face. God needed to test their obedience time and time again. He wanted Israel to wander in the wilderness, so they could become the best version of His people—ready and able to handle everything in their way. He wants the same for us.

The Distraction

In my restless wilderness years as a young mother, I decided to pursue a ministry in music. I had already said "no" to an agent once in my life and now I decided to give it another try. Looking back, I can see all the warning signs. God was maneuvering circumstances to get my attention to pull back, but like a determined toddler, I was rushing full speed ahead.

I had to drive 90 miles to catch a flight to Los Angeles for my audition and the morning started off uneventful. Barreling down the highway, I missed the turnoff to the airport short cut, adding a half hour to my trip. Those were the days before Google Maps. Just in case that wasn't enough of a flashing red light, I hit a stretch of road construction on a two-lane highway. Waiting for a pilot car took a long, seemingly endless, half hour after which we crawled at a snail's pace for over ten miles. Now I was an hour behind and was going to miss my plane. God was trying to get my attention. Do you think I was listening at that point?

When I got to the airport parking lot, my plane was boarding. I sprinted like I was in the Olympics. Getting through the door at the last second, I settled in to my seat thankful I hadn't been left behind. After arriving in LA and breezing through the audition with the new recording company, I happily shelled out the agent fee my husband had borrowed from the bank. I flew back home with visions of my new life swirling in my head. Three months later, with no recording date yet in sight, we received an apologetic letter from the agency saying they had gone bankrupt, and our money (and my dreams) evaporated. Time to take the long way around.

Sister, if you're facing a wilderness in your life, know that God does not have you there to punish you. He is not neglecting you; He hasn't forgotten about you. He knows how you feel; He knows every hurt and every trial that has come your way. God wants you "mature and complete, not lacking anything" (James 1:4). He has bigger and better plans for you, and He is using the wilderness to refine your will. "He is wooing you from the jaws of distress to a spacious place, free from restriction, to the comfort of your table laden with choice food" (Job 36:16). It might feel like you are trudging through a thick quagmire of mud or lost in an endless circle of detours, but your promised land is coming.

The Love Connection: Obey and Remain

Obedience is the path to God for *every* believer. Jesus clarified this is in the New Testament; we see it most vividly in John 14-15. In these chapters we find two key principles:

- If we love God, we *obey* His commands.
- When we *remain* in His love, our life reflects our obedience And our lives "will be even more fruitful" (John 15:2).

Jesus said, "if you love me, you will obey my commands" four times in John 14-15. This is the divine connection God desires: we obey *because* we love (1 John 4:19). God doesn't want us to obey out of fear, but from pure love-fueled desire and trust. And He equipped us to receive that love by cleaning us up, giving us a new heart, and putting His Spirit inside us to help us follow Him (Ez. 36:25-27). Signed, sealed, delivered…we're His.

The Master Gardener

One mistake we can make as believers is to see obedience as a checklist of tasks. Do this: good. Don't do that: bad. But in John 15, we see obedience as the act of "remaining" in God or being continually present with Him. Jesus illustrates this by using an analogy his listeners could easily understand: gardening. He said, "I am the vine; you are the branches. If you remain in me and I in you, you will bear much fruit; apart from me you can do nothing" (John 15:5).

In the first ten verses of John 15, Jesus uses the word *remain* (or some form of it) eleven times. Obedience is not ticking all the boxes and then running off to do our own thing. Obedience that cements a love relationship is about remaining—staying connected to the vine when times are good, when times are bad—because we know the Gardener loves us. And that remaining produces fruit; tangible behaviors that show up in our lives.

Sometimes God cuts off a branch, and we have to grieve the loss of something that is not good for us (John 15:2). God also prunes our fruitful lives so they will be even more fruitful. And sometimes that pruning hurts a little. It's like pinching off the budding blooms on a flowering plant to turn a ho-hum flower into one that stops traffic with its overflowing blooms. I am a branch; He is the loving Master Gardener. He knows which buds to pinch off. When we finally get ahold of the revelation that love thrives in obedience, we are on the path God has marked out for us to run. God knows what we need to do; we need to remain.

Making the Right Choice

The key to unleashing the obedience-love connection is living the reality of God's unfailing love in our everyday lives. A true legacy is formed in the *real* moments of life—times when we think it doesn't matter: When someone pulls into a parking space we are waiting for. When our granddaughter spills her juice on the brand-new carpeting. When you open your home to the new neighbors. When you walk into church and extend a welcoming hand and smile to that young woman who has a baby but no husband. These are the fruits of remaining in God's love.

God's Love Is Unfailing

In order to embed the obedience-love connection in our lives, we must cling to four truths like a bulldog playing tug-of-war with a frayed piece of rope. They are not negotiable. If we implant them in our lives, they will be our GPS as we run our race.

The Four Truths of God's Unfailing Love

Truth #1: God's unfailing love is available to all. In John 3:16, Jesus promises unfailing love to everyone who believes in Him. No strings attached. It's available to us all at our worst and at our best. That saving love is no respecter of persons. It doesn't matter what we've done or what we've accomplished. His love covers it all. "But God demonstrates his own love for us in this: While we were still sinners, Christ died for us" (Rom. 5:8).

Truth #2: God's unfailing love allows us to suffer. We sometimes find it hard to believe that a loving God would allow us to suffer. But Hebrews 12:7-11 teaches that God disciplines those he loves, so they may share in His holiness. The path to sharing in His holiness is sometimes filled with a lot of uncomfortable bud-pinching. But He's a good Father. His loving pruning shears enable us to grow (John 15:1-2).

Truth #3: God's unfailing love is relentless—always pursuing, always with us. In Psalm 139 we see the relentless love of a God. The psalmist asks, "Where can I go from your Spirit? Where can I flee from your presence?" (v. 7). Then we see a list (vv. 8-12) proving that there is absolutely nowhere we can go to get away from God's love, including hiding in the darkness. "The eyes of the LORD are everywhere, keeping watch on the wicked and the good" (Prov. 15:3). You can't escape that ferocious love; and you can't hide from it either.

Truth #4: God's unfailing love is a beautiful mystery. Our culture has a fascination with tangible proof. If I can't see it, touch it, read it, or understand it, I don't believe it. We demand the concrete data. Show me the money! Sisters, God is a mystery. We cannot fully comprehend Him; He cannot be explained with a spreadsheet.

In Paul's letter to the Ephesians he prays that the believers would be rooted and established in love, so they may have power to grasp "how wide and long and high and deep is the love of Christ, and to *know this love that surpasses knowledge*" (Ephesians 3:18-19, emphasis mine). How can we know something that surpasses knowledge? A look at the translation of the Greek word used for "know" and "knowledge" indicates a state of experience not head knowledge. And the word *surpasses* indicates a transcendence or a place beyond. Paul wasn't citing a spiritual address here—a place we could arrive—but a state of constant growth. God is infinite; our minds are finite. Embracing that mystery is a necessary mind-set of keeping our eyes fixed on the finish line.

My prayer for you: I pray that you, being rooted and established in love, would have power together with all the saints to grasp how wide and long and high and deep is the love of Christ, and *to know this love that surpasses knowledge* that you may be filled to the measure of all the fullness of God (Eph. 3:17-19).

DAY ONE: DIGGING DEEPER

Pray and ask for God's wisdom as you consider what stood out to you in this week's reading. Write your thoughts in your study journal. Look intently into God's Word, and you will be blessed in what you do (James 1:25).

1. Read Exodus 19:5-6 and Romans 7:7. Why does God ask us to obey His commands? What is the connection between love and obedience?
2. Read John 14:15-21. Why does Jesus put such an important emphasis on obedience? What is the Holy Spirit's role in helping us obey?
3. Read John 15:1-10. What does it mean to remain in God? What does God do with branches in our lives that bear no fruit? What might that look like?

   Why does God prune our "fruitful branches"?

4. Of the four essential "truths" about God's love in this chapter, which is the most difficult for you to experience? Why do you think that is?
5. Read Hebrews 12:4-13 in *The Message* translation. Why is God "training us to live His holy best"?
6. How does God's training "pay off handsomely"?

DAY TWO: LEGACY BUILDING BLOCKS
FINDING YOUR COMMUNITIES OF INFLUENCE

Truth Fact: A woman finishing well sees the potential for influence wherever she goes.

Our lives are filled with groups of people we regularly move in and out of. We may not know their names or have a relationship with them beyond the context in which we meet, but we can develop a level of influence with them that reveals God's love. These are our communities of influence.

1. In your journal, make a list of anyone you see regularly in the situations below. You may or may not know their names. If you don't, just write a descriptive word or two that identifies how you cross paths.
   a. People I interact with in a club or hobby setting (Bunco group, card groups, book club, golf, tennis, walking, swimming).
   b. Service providers I see regularly (grocery store clerks, baristas, home care providers, mail and delivery people, hair stylists, house cleaners)
   c. People at church I visit with but don't see socially outside of church.
2. Circle the people above you can't attach a name to. Make a point to find out each person's name and start calling them by name when you see them. Dale Carnegie, author of *How to Win Friends and Influence People*, wrote: "A person's name is to him or her the sweetest and most important sound in any language." Make their day, open a door. Pray for God to give you greater influence with everyone above.

3. If your communities of influence are few (maybe just one or two), add a prayer request to this list asking God to widen your influence. He may ask you to step outside your comfort zone a little and get more involved. Or it might mean just paying more attention to the people who are already in your day.

DAY THREE: FIRST THINGS FIRST

1. Make a commitment to pray for everyone in your circle of influence and your communities of influence this week.
2. Make an effort this week to find out the names of those in your communities of influence that you do not know. Start calling them by name.

CHAPTER THREE

GETTING YOUR BIRTHRIGHT RIGHT

SET YOUR HEART

"How great is the love the Father has lavished on us that we should be called children of God! And that is what we are!"

—1 John 3:1

"Since then you have been raised with Christ, set your hearts on things above, where Christ is seated at the right hand of God. Set your minds on things above not on earthly things"

—Colossians 3:1-2

The Cinderella Wake-Up Call

Cinderella had forgotten who she was. When her father was alive, she was his only child and his only heir. But when he died, her evil stepmother demoted her status to maid. Yet, Cinderella held out hope that someday her prince would come and sweep her away to live happily ever after. When a public invitation to a grand ball at the castle came, she saw her chance to meet the prince. She hustled to the attic to find a dress from her mother's trunk of old clothes. As she was rummaging through the trunk, she heard the click of the door's bolt sliding into place behind her. But even a locked door could not keep her from her destiny. Fairy godmother to the rescue! She reminded Cinderella who she was and began waving her magic wand, transforming Cinderella into a princess. Well, you know the rest.

It's one thing to sing, "I'm a child of the King" and another thing to live like one. We need a Cinderella wake-up call to unbolt the door keeping us captive. To claim our birthright, we have to be tenacious. We need to go beyond wishing, shed our slave girl garb, get decked out in our royal robe, and slip our foot into that glass slipper.

In the next two chapters we are going to be studying the core of our challenge to claim that new family identity by *setting our hearts and minds on things above, not on things in this life* (Col. 3:1-2).

This Is Us

Our new family identity as a child of God begins the moment we acknowledge we are sinners in need of God, believe that Jesus died for our personal sins, and turn our lives over to Him. Once we cross that line, we have a new family status. Belief begins in the heart. When we "set our hearts on things above," this is what we're staking our belief on:

- God has called us by name and redeemed us from death (Eph. 1:7, Gal. 3:13-14)
- His Spirit in us witnesses that we are his child (Rom 8:16)
- We are children by faith (Gal. 3:26, John 1:12)
- He made us and we are his (1 John 3:1-2, Ps. 139:13-16)

Believing all that God has done for you is the first hurdle in embracing your family identity. Never forget who you are. Never forget that God, by His amazing grace and mercy, brought you out of whatever pit you were in and gave you a firm place to stand in a new family (Ps. 40:2).

The Family Promises – Our Legacy

But what does it mean to be a child of God? When we were growing up, chances are we knew what it meant to be a child of our earthly families—how we were supposed to dress, where we went for holidays, which sports teams we rooted for on the weekends, what we had for supper on Friday nights, and the list goes on. But what about our new family? What does it look like to be a member of God's family?

In Ephesians 1:3-14, Paul presents a perfect picture of our family legacy. I've personalized this master list of family benefits to make it sticky. Speak it out loud daily; it will help cement the truths into your heart. These truths belong to each of us who are in Christ:

- I am blessed in the heavenly realms with every spiritual blessing in Christ (v.3).
- I am chosen to be holy and blameless in His sight. He has forgiven my sins (v.4).
- I am His adopted child (v.5).
- He has redeemed me from death (v.7).
- He has lavished His grace upon me (v.8).
- He has made known to me the mystery of His will (v.9).
- I have been chosen, and He has a plan for me (vs.11-12).
- I am marked with a seal guaranteeing my inheritance. I am God's possession (v.13-14).

This is your God-given legacy. Everything on that list. No one can take it away from you; it is your heritage.

Setting our Minds Above to Leave the Past Behind

Now we know what it means to *be* a child of God. But what does it look like to *live like* a child of God? First, we must drop some of the heavy baggage we've been dragging around. It's slowing you down.

In Colossians 3, Paul didn't tell us just to set our minds on *things above*. He also told us not to set our minds on *earthly things*. He gave us a list of earthly things we are supposed to leave behind, and he put on exclamation on the list with three important words: *put to death*. Anything that tethers you to this world has to die (v. 5). Behaviors that are part of our old family relationship: sexual immorality, impurity, lust, evil desires, and greed. Those we can all agree on. But what about those little ensnaring things we don't think are that harmful? Anger, rage, malice, slander, filthy language, and lying (vs. 8-9). Yup, those too. They all need to go.

And you can't just take off the old clothes. You would have no identity—you'd be naked. You have to put on the new clothes. That is the "set your minds on things above" part. Paul wrote the Ephesians:

> You were taught with regard to your former way of life to put off your old self, which is being corrupted by its deceitful desires; to be made new in the attitude of your minds; and to put on the new self, created to be like God in true righteousness and holiness. (Ephesians 4:22-24)

We need to take off the old, worn out clothes smelling of fear and hopelessness, wash off the dirty sweat of striving to be accepted, and put on the fresh, crisp garments of grace, forgiveness, and trust (Col. 3:5-11).

But putting things to death takes a constant effort. Some days a nagging sinful behavior we thought was behind us pops up again. Paul knew this dilemma all too well, and we can hear his frustration in his letter to the Romans: "For I do not do the good I want to do, but the evil I don't want to do—this I keep on doing" (Romans 7:19). But keep moving forward, one foot in front of the other. Call on God for His mercy and grace and keep on. God will honor your perseverance. You will make it.

The Struggle is Real

In the same letter Paul wrote, "do not let sin reign in your mortal body so that you do not obey its evil desires" (Romans 6:12). That is the struggle, isn't it? Living in these pesky mortal bodies. Our bodies and minds have memories. Memories of pleasure, memories of old habits, memories of old hurts—they don't automatically disappear when we are saved.

One of the biggest roadblocks to taking off the old self and putting on the new self, is overcoming a painful past. Some of us grew up in difficult circumstances. Your path to setting your heart on things above may involve much-needed forgiveness, starting with yourself. And sometimes that forgiveness is a journey, not a one-time declaration. And all journeys start with one step.

In *Breaking Free*, Beth Moore says we must be willing to take a look back for purposes of moving on, not to cast blame:

> "Sometimes we're willing to criticize what happened before us, but are we willing to take the challenge of positively affecting those after us? The little slice of time God offers each generation is a trust. Those before us who were unfaithful with their trust will be held accountable, *but we're still here.* We still have a chance to positively affect the generations that follow us."[2]

A New Heart

We can have a positive influence on the generations after us even if those before us left a legacy of pain. Make the most of your slice of time. You are still here! Some days it feels like the rusty chains of our past will never fall off. If you've been given a legacy that requires some healing, please don't hesitate to get help. There is no shame in wanting to rid yourself of those heavy chains. "It is for freedom that Christ has set us free" (Gal. 5:1). God is a chain-breaker and a way-maker, and oftentimes he uses wise people to help us heal.

Unfortunately, our past is not obliterated by some wand-waving spell like in a *Harry Potter* movie. One of my favorite ways to bond my new family legacy to my heart is to recite that first-person paraphrase from Ephesians we saw earlier in this chapter. Speaking those verses regularly helps the truth make the journey from my head to my heart. I encourage you to write it out, memorize it, declare it, own it, and live it:

> I am blessed in the heavenly realms with every spiritual blessing in Christ. I am chosen to be holy and blameless in His sight. He has forgiven my sins. I am His adopted child.

He has redeemed from death and forgiven all my sins. He has lavished His grace upon me. He has made known to me the mystery of His will. I have been chosen and He has a plan for me. I am marked with a seal guaranteeing my inheritance. I am God's possession.

---

[2] Beth Moore, *Breaking Free* (Nashville: B&H Books, 2007), 109, emphasis added.

My prayer for you: I pray that the eyes of your heart may be enlightened so that you may know the hope to which you've been called, the riches of your glorious inheritance in the saints, and the incomparably great power for those who believe (Eph. 1:18-19).

DAY ONE: DIGGING DEEPER

Pray and ask for God's wisdom as you consider what stood out to you in this week's reading. Write your thoughts in your study journal. Look intently into God's Word, and you will be blessed in what you do (Jas. 1:25).

In your *Digging Deeper* studies, it may be helpful to have a Bible concordance or other study helps handy. You can find a wealth of study tools on the website BibleStudyTools.com.

1. Read Ephesians 1:3-14. Do you struggle with any of these "spiritual blessings in Christ"? Using a concordance or online search, look for three additional Bible verses that confirm that blessing you're wrestling with. Write these verses in your journal and ask God to give you guidance about how to make this blessing your own.

2. Read the following verses and write your thoughts on what each of these verses says to you about setting your mind on things above:

    Romans 8:16:

    1 Corinthians 2:16:

    Philippians. 2:5:

3. Is the legacy you inherited one that you want to change? What steps can you take today to start the journey to leave the past behind?

4. Read 2 Timothy 2:15. Why is it important for us to be reading and studying the Bible on a regular basis?

5. Read the list of behaviors in Colossians 3:5-8. Is there something on that list that continually trips you up? Ask God to help you put it to death in your life.

DAY TWO: LEGACY BUILDING BLOCKS
THE POWER OF THE SPOKEN WORD

Truth Fact: A woman finishing well knows that the Word of God is alive and active; sharper than any double-edged sword and judges the thoughts and attitude of the heart (Heb. 4:12).

A right word spoken at the right time can be life-giving (Pr. 15:23). Learning to infuse your daily life with God's Word requires familiarity. Speaking God's Word is like fertilizing the soft ground of our hearts as we plant each truth. The more God's truth takes root, the more our hearts get set, and the more those words bear fruit in our daily lives.

In our study we are not just going to read and memorize the Word, we are going to master how to speak it with power. We will learn how to take Scripture, put it in the first person, and speak it as an affirming prayer.

1. Read the following Scriptures and note what each says about the words we speak:
   a. James 3:6:
   b. Prov. 15:4:
   c. Prov. 15:23:
   d. Prov. 18:21:
2. What are some other creative ways we can keep Scripture in the forefront of our daily lives?
3. Read Colossians 3:16. What are some ways we can let the Word of God dwell in us richly?
4. Find a favorite verse in the Bible that resonates with you about who you are in Christ and personalize it—write it in the first person (I, my mine, etc.). Write it out on an index card. Be sure and put the scripture reference (chapter and verse) on the card as well.

   Here are some examples to get you going:

   a. Philippians 4:13
   b. 1 Cor. 10:13
   c. Philippians 1:6

    d.   1 Jn. 5:14-15

    e.   Romans 8:28

5.   After you've written out your Bible verse on a card, find a place to post it where you can see it regularly. I call these Refrigerator Verses because that's one common place we visit everyday. By posting the verse on your refrigerator door (or microwave door or bathroom mirror), it becomes a visual reminder to speak the verse out loud every time you see it.

Read that verse every time you pass it until you can speak it without reading the card. After you've committed that verse to memory, write a new verse on a new index card and repeat the process. Tip: Keep the memorized index cards in your purse. Pull them out every once in a while and read them when you're in a waiting room or standing in a long line at the grocery store.

DAY THREE: FIRST THINGS FIRST
WAKE-UP CALL & WATER

It's time to start tackling our First Things First routine with the **Wake-Up Call** and a glass of **Water**.

1.   Put together your **wake-up call** for tomorrow morning:

The purpose of a wake-up call is to take advantage of that first conscious moment of the morning before you get out of bed and turn your heart toward God. The wake-up call is a short, heartfelt prayer thanking Him for the new day and committing it to His purpose. Say it every morning before you get out of bed. Before your feet hit the floor. Before you pick up your phone. Before your mind engages elsewhere. Start tomorrow.

Here's an example: "God, You are good. Thank You, Lord, for this new day. I ask you to lead me and guide me today in the way I should go. Bring people into my life today that you want me to influence. Keep my heart and mind fixed on You."

Keep it short, keep it simple, and pray it fervently every morning before you get up. If you need a reminder, put a sticky note on your bathroom mirror or wherever you will see it right away in the morning.

2. Tomorrow morning, **drink a glass of water before you drink or eat anything else**. I leave a full glass of water in my bathroom every night so the water is room temperature in the morning. I drink it right after I get out of bed. Your body has gone six to ten hours (depending on how long you sleep) without any hydration. Before you start pouring in the caffeine or sugar (or herbal tea), drink at least eight good gulps of water. Note: There may be a medical or personal issue why you can't do this. I get it. Give it your best shot if you're able.

   Why drink water first thing? Here are eight good reasons via Life Hack.

   a. Helps rid the body of toxins that build up during dehydration
   b. Improves your metabolism
   c. Helps you maintain a healthy weight
   d. Alleviates heartburn and indigestion
   e. Promotes healthy skin
   f. Gives you healthier hair
   g. Helps prevent bladder and kidney stones
   h. Strengthens your immune system

3. Practice your first two "W"s every day. 'Nuff said.

CHAPTER FOUR

POWER-UP FOR BATTLE
SETTING YOUR MIND

"For though we live in the world, we do not wage war as the world does. The weapons we fight with are not the weapons of the world. On the contrary, they have divine power to demolish strongholds. We demolish arguments and every pretension that sets itself up against God, and we take captive every thought and make it obedient to Christ."

—2 Corinthians 10:3-5

"Therefore, put on the full armor of God, so that when the day of evil comes, you may be able to stand your ground, and after you have done everything, to stand. Stand firm then, with the belt of truth buckled around your waist, with the breastplate of righteousness in place, and with your feet fitted with the readiness that comes from the gospel of peace. In addition to all this, take up the shield of faith, with which you can extinguish all the flaming arrows of the evil one. Take the helmet of salvation and the sword of the Spirit, which is the word of God."

-Ephesians 6:13-17

You've Got the Power

The Hoover Dam is magnificent. Sitting on the border between Arizona and Nevada, it can generate an annual 4.5 billion kilowatt hours of electricity to serve the needs of nearly 8 million people in Arizona, southern California, and southern Nevada. And how does all that electricity get produced? The dam's gates release a measured amount of water through pipes and turbines that turn the dam into a giant battery. And what happens if that water is stopped? Eight million people will be fumbling in the dark. The *ability* to produce the power is still there, but the *process* of producing power ceases to exist.

When God redeemed us, all His power and promises became part of our family legacy. To activate that power, we need to keep plugged in to the source (Col. 3:2-4). The same power that raised Jesus from the dead (Eph. 1:18-20) is available to us. The same power that flattened the walls of Jericho at a trumpet blast. The same power that breathed life into a pile of dust and a human being was formed.

The Power Struggle

There are two natures struggling for power within us: the spiritual nature that accompanies our birthright as a child of God and the sinful nature we were born with. In Romans 7:21-25, Paul describes the battle within:

> So I find this law at work: Although I want to do good, evil is right there with me. For in my inner being I delight in God's law; but I see another law at work in me, waging war against the law of my mind and making me a prisoner of the law of sin at work within me. What a wretched man I am! Who will rescue me from the body that is subject to death? Thanks be to God, who delivers me through Jesus Christ our Lord! So then, I myself in my mind am a slave to God's law, but in the sinful nature a slave to the law of sin.

This is our daily skirmish: keeping plugged in to the spiritual power source and denying the old nature any spark that might get the turbines whirling. We are warriors, and warriors need rules of engagement, or battle mind-sets, complete with weapons of destruction to fight our hounding enemy. Make no mistake; your enemy is real, and he is not wandering aimlessly. He has a plan to keep us powerless.

The Man Behind the Curtain

Do you remember the scene in *The Wizard of Oz* where Dorothy and her three companions returned to Oz with the wicked witch's broom? After asking the wizard to make good on his promise to help them, the angry wizard head, spewing fire and smoke, told them to go away. As the angry exchange continued, Dorothy's dog, Toto, scampered to a nearby booth and pulled aside the curtain where the real "wizard" was pulling levers and frantically pressing buttons. As he feverishly tried to regain his composure after being discovered, he kept yelling into his microphone, "pay no attention to that man behind the curtain!"

That is a perfect picture of our enemy. He is the man behind the curtain, pulling levers and using smoke and mirrors to distract us from God. He is not omnipresent, so he can't be everywhere at once—or even two places at once. He is not omnipotent; his power pales next to the One who parted the Red Sea. But he is orchestrating a large army whose main purpose is to wear us down. We need some battle mind-sets.

The Battle Mindsets – Five Essential Truths

A true warrior understands the enemy's tactics. I've identified five essential truths to give you a battle mindset we need to defeat the "evil rulers and authorities of the unseen world" (Eph. 6:12, NLT).

1. *Understand who we're fighting and where the battle takes place.*

"For though we live in the world, we do not wage war as the world does. The weapons we fight with are not the weapons of this world" (2 Cor. 10:3-4).

We live *in* the world, but we're not fighting according to the world's rules or on the world's turf.

How many times do we blame what we can see when trouble comes rushing at us? We blame our boss, our elderly parent, that bad stock investment, that drunk driver, my cranky neighbor, or that cancer that's invaded my body. Certainly people, places, and things can bring trials and tragedy. But they are not the enemy. The real battle for our heart and soul is taking place on unseen battle-grounds and is against Satan and his dark and scheming spiritual powers. Know where the battle is taking place. Know your true enemy. When life throws a curve ball, remember who the pitcher is.

2) *The battle belongs to God not us.*

David was an unlikely hero. As a matter of fact, he was so unlikely that his father sent him out to watch the sheep when the prophet Samuel came looking for a future king. And later, when King Saul told David he was no match for Goliath, David recounted escapades of killing lions and bears with his bare hands. He wanted a shot at the mammoth Philistine.

When Saul gave in, David stepped up to the plate. He stood in the hot sun, sweat trickling down his face, with nothing more than his staff, five smooth stones, and a slingshot. Goliath, a nine-foot giant, was decked out in almost eighty pounds of bronze armor from head to foot. Insulted at the sight of puny, armor-less David, Goliath started talking smack to the young shepherd boy. Famous last words. David set Goliath straight:

> "You come against me with sword and spear and javelin, but I come against you in the name of the LORD Almighty, the God of the armies of Israel, whom you have defiled. This day the LORD will deliver you into my hands." (1 Samuel 17:45-46)

The towering giant had heard enough and started running forward to squash the little big mouth. And what did David do? He "ran quickly toward the battle line to meet him" (1 Sam. 17:48). David's confidence was in His divine Defender not his size or weapons.

3) *Live in the armor of God.*

The armor of God is not something we run and grab when we see smoke on the horizon. When Paul said, "Put on the armor of God" (Eph. 6:11), that was meant to be a one-time permanent act. The armor is something we live in not something we take on and off like a set of clothes. Don't underestimate the enemy. There won't be a knock on the door when the forces of hell decide to show up. Your spiritual weapons have the power to immobilize any enemy attack, anywhere, any time. Be ready.

In Ephesians 6:14-17, Paul lists the pieces of armor and weapons we have as children of God. Become familiar with each piece and its purpose:

- "Stand firm with the *belt of truth* buckled at your waist" (v. 14). Our midsection and lower back house the muscular power core of the body. Biomechanically, the core supports every physical movement we make. A weak core easily gives way to injury when the body undergoes physical stress. God's *truth* is our power core in battle. The truth about who God is, the truth about who we are, and the truth about our enemy.

- Stand firm "with the *breastplate of righteousness* in place" (v. 14). The breastplate protects our most important asset, physically as well as spiritually: the heart. Just as our physical heart continually pumps life-giving blood to every vessel in our body, our spiritual heart is our wellspring of life-giving connection to God (Pr. 4:23).

- Keep "your feet fitted with the readiness that comes from the *gospel of peace*" (v. 15). God wants us to be ready and willing to go wherever He asks and do whatever He asks us to do. And the Greek word *hetoimos*, used for readiness here, means "to be prepared." Those shoes of peace need to be on our feet, not sitting in the closet. We need to be ready to go.

- "Take up the *shield of faith* with which you can extinguish all the flaming arrows of the evil one" (v. 16). The enemy shoots arrows from multiple locations and angles. The shield of faith is one of two movable pieces of armor. It gives us 360-degree protection against those arrows before they hit their mark. Carrying a shield of faith means believing in what God can do over what we can see.

- "Take the *helmet of salvation*" (v. 17). Knowing that we are redeemed and loved by God protects our minds from doubt and fear. Trust in Him alone.

- Take *"the sword of the Spirit*, which is the word of God"* (v. 17). The second movable weapon is the sword of God's word—a truth for every occasion, every attack the enemy throws your way. The

Word of God has the power to separate the enemy's slyest deception from God's truth (Heb. 4:12). Be a woman who learns how to rightly divide the word of truth (2 Tim. 2:15).

- "And *pray* in the Spirit on all occasions." The Greek word for time (on all occasions) in this verse is *kairos*. God's eternal time clock. It's not the limited 24-hour day of *hromos* time. Think of something that is ongoing and always "in season." In other words, not just something you do as an appointed task, but a lifestyle. Beyond the constraints of time. "Never stop praying" (1 Thes. 5:17, New Living Translation). God has his own time zone.

Live in the armor of God. Everyday. And be alert. We never know where and when the next clash will come. But we do know it is a steady onslaught. Weapons up!

4) *Trust what you know.*

Remember the battle is spiritual and even though it looks like that health issue has the upper hand, you cannot trust in what you see, only in what you know.

Let's revisit Joshua right after the Israelites crossed the Jordan into the promised land. There was no more manna. They were finally home. Imagine how overwhelmed they were when, after their tenuous journey, they found out their first task was to conquer Jericho, a magnificent city whose walls loomed large on the horizon.

According to historic accounts, Jericho's defenses were three-tiered. First there was a trench around the city that sloped up to a stone retaining wall that stood about twelve feet high. Behind that wall was another steep incline that led to the city wall. This final wall was six feet thick, made of mud bricks, and loomed twenty feet high. Together, the three tiers were about the size of a ten-story building. But the Israelites needed to trust in what they knew. What they saw looked overwhelming.

We wonder how many of them wanted to just stay by the shores of the Jordan and hunt for those gigantic juicy grape clusters the spies had brought back on tent poles. Maybe Joshua had misheard God about annihilating the inhabitants of the land? And then to add to their apprehension, Joshua unfolded a wacky battle plan that included just marching around the city walls for six days and blowing trumpets. The people in Jericho were probably not scared (yawn), but the Israelites might have been.

Do you think they were getting weary after six days of marching? Frightened? Knowing the truth of God's Word doesn't always calm the feisty emotions or ease our physical challenges. On the morning of the seventh day there were probably a few sweaty palms, upset stomachs, and extra trips to the outhouse. But they set out again based on what they knew: the battle was not theirs, but God's.

> On the seventh day they rose early, at the dawn of the day and marched around the city in the same manner, except that on that day they circled the city seven times. The seventh time around, when the priests had sounded the trumpet blast, Joshua commanded the army, "Shout! For the LORD has given you the city!" ... When the trumpets sounded, the army shouted, and at the sound of the trumpet, when the men gave a loud shout, the wall collapsed; so every man charged straight in, and they took the city. (Joshua 6:15-20)

Can you imagine the elation and relief as the Israelites climbed over the rubble of broken walls to take the city God had promised them? That day they learned what it meant to obey God in the face of fear.

5) *Our victory has already been secured.*

This is hard to latch on to when you're *in* the fray and arrows are zinging by your ears. We need to head *into* battle with this mind-set firmly in place. No questions. No doubts. This takes steely courage—the kind of boldness that unexpected arrows can't dismantle. When Joshua was preparing the Israelites to cross the Red Sea, he told them four times to "be strong and courageous." He promised the Lord would be with them wherever they went (Josh. 1:9). He had no doubts. And that courage penetrated the entire nation of Israel as they responded, "whatever you command us we will do, and wherever you send us we will go" (Josh. 1:16).

Jesus has already confirmed the enemy's powerlessness at the cross (Col. 2:15, Eph. 1:20-22). And the enemy is powerless against an armored-up Christian.

Jars of Clay

Before I send you off marching to war with a feeling of immortality, let's stop and remember our mortality for a moment. God has given us some powerful spiritual weapons, but they are housed in our imperfect jar of clay (2 Cor. 4:7). It is so easy to get discouraged when we face battles. But Paul actually found encouragement in his mortality by remembering that even when he was struck down, he was not destroyed:

> But we have this treasure in jars of clay to show that this all-surpassing power is from God and not from us. We are hard pressed on ever side, but not crushed; perplexed, but not in despair; persecuted, but not abandoned; struck down, but not destroyed…Therefore we do not lose heart. Though outwardly we are wasting away, yet inwardly we are being renewed day by day. For our light and momentary troubles are achieving for us an eternal glory that far outweighs them all. So we fix our eyes not on what is seen, but on what is unseen. For what is seen is temporary, but what is unseen is eternal. (2 Cor. 4:7-18)

Yes, we are mortal. Yes, our bodies are aging. But our spirits are getting stronger every day. And there is something beyond this life that is worth fighting for: an eternal glory that far outweighs any trouble and any battle that comes our way. That is our battle legacy. Keep fighting. God does not want to be your last resort; He wants to be your first line of defense.

My prayer for you: God, we pray you would enlighten the eyes of all our hearts so that we may know You and Your incomparably great power for us. That power is the *same* power that raised Jesus from the dead. Help us to know the power in us is greater than the power coming against us (Eph. 1:17-20).

DAY ONE: DIGGING DEEPER

Pray and ask for God's wisdom as you consider what stood out to you in this week's reading. Write your thoughts in your study journal. Look intently into God's Word, and you will be blessed in what you do (Jas. 1:25).

1. Read Ephesians 1:17-21. What does Paul compare the power within us to in verse 19? Why is it important to remember the matchless quality of the power residing in us when it comes to fighting the enemy?
2. Are there battles you fight on a regular basis? Which of those is most difficult for you to "believe what you know and not what you see" and why?
3. Look again at the individual pieces of God's armor in Ephesians 6:10-17. Is there a piece or pieces that are difficult for you to remember to put on? Why do you think that is?
4. What kinds of things can you be doing to help "buckle the belt of truth at your waist" (Eph. 6:14)?
5. Read Col. 3:1-2 and Rom. 8:6. What does a Spirit-controlled mind look like to you? How do you keep your mind set on things above?
6. Read 2 Corinthians 4:7-18. Put together a two-column chart in your journal and fill in the corresponding "spiritual benefit" next to each difficulty we face in battle. Look over the chart one line at a time. What kind of picture does this paint about spiritual battle?

Difficulty	Spiritual Benefit
Hard pressed on every side (vs. 8)	
Perplexed (vs. 8)	
Persecuted (vs. 9)	
Struck down (vs. 9)	

DAY TWO: LEGACY BUILDING BLOCKS
THE PHILIPPIANS 4:8 TEST

Truth Fact: A woman finishing well makes choices that keep her heart and mind connected to God (Col. 3:1-2).

> Whatever is true, whatever is noble, whatever is right, whatever is pure, whatever is lovely, whatever is admirable, if anything is excellent or praiseworthy—think on these things. (Phil. 4:8)

Garbage in, garbage out. Even though you won't find those exact words in the Bible, there are plenty of verses that support the idea that whatever occupies our mind and heart will shape who we are. We make hundreds of choices every day: what we eat, where we go, who we hang out with, what we watch on TV, what we read, and more. Each one of those choices has the power to pull our minds away from God to focus on distractions down here in the trenches.

> "The eye is the lamp of the body. If your eyes are healthy, your whole body will be full of light. But if your eyes are unhealthy, your whole body will be full of darkness." (Mat. 6:22-23)

The Amplified Bible uses the phrase "spiritually blind" in verse 23 instead of the word *unhealthy*. Some of the poor choices we are making are the result of blind spots.

Am I participating in a good old-fashioned gossip session with friends at Starbucks? What about that movie everybody wants to go to but probably is a little too steamy or salty for my comfort level? What about that TV program that has a constant parade of sexual escapades or graphic violence? Or that guy at work that smiles at you and complements your wardrobe selection everyday? And now he's sitting alone at lunch.

I know I am tiptoeing on tricky ground here. Everyone's idea of what is true, noble, and right will vary. But breathe easy—I'm not going to make a do-this-don't-do-that list for you. That's your job. The important thing is you *should* have such a list in your head that you put together with the help of the Holy Spirit. It defines your intentions, pure and simple. And intention is the foundation of obedience. Know where the chinks in your armor are.

We're bombarded with evil at every turn. We need to be steadfast and keep our eyes open for anything that pulls our mind away from God. This extends to who we hang out with, where we go, how we spend our money, what we watch, and more. Let's start with the Philippians 4:8 Test as a guidepost. I think *The Message* has the best checklist:

> Summing it all up, friends, I'd say you'll do best by filling your minds and meditating on things true, noble, reputable, authentic, compelling, gracious—the best, not the worst; the beautiful, not the ugly; things to praise, not things to curse. (Phil. 4:8, MSG)

1. Start by praying for God to show you those people, places, TV shows, books, movies, music, friends, and hobbies that are drawing you away from Him. Be open to listening to the Holy Spirit. Ask God to poke you *before* you make a choice you're not sure is best. Ask Him to reveal your blind spots. Write Philippians 4:8 on an index card and tape it next to your TV. Having that reminder in your eyesight will make you think twice before you watch that iffy show. Consider memorizing this verse so you'll always have it with you when temptation pops up. And remember—your iffy shows may not be my iffy shows. This is a no judgment zone.

2. Make a list of the people, places, and things you feel are drawing your heart away from God. Pray for God to help you replace those activities and people with something or someone that is true, noble, right, pure, and gracious. Put this list in your journal and pray for it regularly.

   Word of warning: This process will take discernment so ask God for it. Follow His lead. Just start by weeding out those things that you *know* draw your heart away from God. Exercise wisdom so you don't become overwhelmed and discouraged. God knows what needs to be done—trust Him. At first, it may feel a little bit like staring at a dessert case loaded with your favorite cupcakes when you're on a diet. If you're giving up toxic friendships, for instance, you could feel guilty or disconnected for a while. But perseverance will "finish its work" (James 1:2-4). God will honor your commitment and hold you tighter. It is always worth it.

DAY THREE: FIRST THINGS FIRST
THE WORD – A SWORD OF MANY COLORS

The Word of God is the third "W" in First Things First. We are so blessed to live in a time when we have God's Word available in so many forms. And now that we have smartphones and tablets, we can have the Bible at our fingertips wherever we go.

In part two of this study we'll learn how to interact with God's Word daily. Right now I'd like to introduce the third "W" to help you become familiar with the many electronic forms of Bibles and reading plans available online. In this lesson, you'll need your smartphone or tablet device and your computer.

1. If you have a smartphone or a device such as an iPad, Samsung Galaxy Tab, or Kindle Fire, you can download the YouVersion Holy Bible app directly from your device's app store. It is free. Make sure you search and download the "YouVersion" Holy Bible app.

2. If you don't have any of the devices listed above, but have a computer, you can access an online version of the app at https://bible.com This version has all the bells and whistle of the application for phones and devices—just not the portability. Access it now and bookmark it on your web browser.

The YouVersion Bible application is a comprehensive digital Bible resource. It houses almost eighteen hundred different Bible versions in over twelve hundred languages. It also includes a word-search function that is similar to a concordance. And, you can turn on an audio function to listen to the Scriptures. Best of all, it contains hundreds of daily reading plans on every book of the Bible and topic you can think of—many written by your favorite Christian writers.

3. After you download the app and set up a free account with your email, spend a few minutes getting familiar with the app's home screen. Some things you will find there:
   a. The **Read** tab will allow you to search the Bible by chapter and verse in any version of the Bible you want.
   b. The **Search** tab will help you find verses that contain certain words or phrases. You can also search by topic there.

c. The **Plans** tab houses hundreds of devotional reading plans you can do alone or with friends. Click on that tab. Explore the various plans available. Do a search of a topic that interests you.

4. Another electronic reading plan source is **The First 5 app** from Proverbs 31 Ministries. I've done several of their reading plans and highly recommend them. You can find out more about their resources online at https://first5.org. You can also search for their app on your phone or device's app store. If you don't have a smart device, you can sign up for reading plans on their website.

CHAPTER FIVE

REMEMBER, REMEMBER
FORGET NOT ALL HIS BENEFITS

"Praise the LORD, O my soul, and forget not his benefits—who forgives all your sins and heals all your diseases, who redeems your life from the pit and crowns you with love and compassion, who satisfies your desires with good things so that your youth is renewed like the eagle's."

—Psalm 103:2-5

"Let each generation tell its children of your mighty acts; let them proclaim your power."

—Psalm 145:4 (NLT)

If You Build It, They Will Remember

Benjamin Franklin said, "When you don't remember, you soon forget." And when you soon forget, those events that strengthened your faith become abandoned, crumbling historical markers on the side of the road. Our legacy grows by purposely remembering and recalling the stories of how God shows up in our lives. We need to put on our work gloves and start building some roadside monuments.

The psalmist describes the cycle of forgetfulness that plagued the Jews in their journey out of Egypt: "When our Fathers were in Egypt, they gave no thought to your miracles; they did not remember your many kindnesses and they rebelled by the sea, the Red Sea" (Ps. 106:7). Do you see the progression? They gave no thought; they did not remember; they rebelled. It's a slippery slope that starts with indifference. Today, we might say, "Meh."

We wonder how anyone could say "meh" to the parting of the Red Sea. But we see what happened next to God's chosen people: "They soon forgot what He had done and did not wait for His counsel. In the desert they gave in to their craving; in the wasteland they put God to the test" (vv. 13-14).

Forgetting is a greenhouse for the seeds of rebellion. In this chapter we'll explore the biblical teaching of remembrance: why it's foundational to establishing a lasting legacy and how it keeps us connected to the reality that God is with us and is leading us where we should go.

Connecting the Generational Dots

"But from everlasting to everlasting the LORD's love is with those who fear him, and his righteousness with their children's children—with those who keep his covenant and remember to obey his precepts." Ps. 103:17-18

Remembering what God has done for us might be the single biggest key to passing on a legacy of faith. There is nothing as powerful as a story, a celebration, an answered prayer request, or a visual reminder to help us keep connected to what God has done, is doing, and will do. Passing on what God has done is the glue that keeps Him close and personal. Remembering is the proof that God's love is with us always (Heb. 13:5-6).

My mother's siblings all wanted their ashes scattered on a family member's ranch in Wyoming. I remember the windy day when my mother and I helped scatter her brother's ashes on a hill overlooking the ranch. I also remember hanging on to my frail mother on that windy hill—the ravages of dementia already creeping into her body—afraid the gusts may blow her away.

So after my mom's death my sister and I made the long trip to Wyoming to honor our mother's wishes. The wind was blowing just as hard that day, but this time it was my sister and I holding on to each other tightly. Not because we were worried about the wind or the sheer edge of the cliff, but because our mother had been a woman of force in our lives. After we took turns scattering her ashes and bidding her a final farewell, my sister suggested we pick up a rock or two as a memory of that day.

We took our time hunting for just the perfect stones to take home. I wanted one flat enough so I could write a date and small epitaph on mine. My sister gathered a few extra for our children and her garden at home. My white quartz rock sits on the desk where I write. It is a visual reminder of God's blessing in my life. My mom is always with me—sometimes still correcting my grammar but always smiling and laughing.

Sometimes We Need a Reminder

We save our wedding dresses, our baby's first pair of shoes, and the worn out T-shirt from our first family vacation—all designed to visually stimulate memories. And the Old Testament Israelites were no different. In Numbers, God impressed on Moses the importance of remembering by giving him a set of sewing instructions:

> Throughout the generations to come you are to make tassels on the corners of your garments, with a blue cord on each tassel. You will have these tassels to look at and so you will remember all the commands of the LORD." (Num. 15:38-39)

Have you ever had a piece of clothing with tassels? There's no missing them when they go by. Their movement draws the eye. And who knew God was into fashion? So much of our time and effort is focused on our hectic daily lives. We need help remembering what we can't afford to forget as we go through our days.

Forget Not All His Benefits

In Psalm 103 we see three different types of remembrances David practiced. What God had done, what He is doing now, and what He will do.

What He has done – *"Praise the Lord, my soul, and forget not all his benefits—who forgives all your sins and heals all your diseases, who redeems your life from the pit, and crowns you with love and compassion"* *(vv. 2-4)*

In these verses, David reminds himself what God has done for him. Remembering what Jesus has done for us personally builds the core of our connection to God. Remembering seeds hope and hope builds perseverance.

What He is doing – *"[Praise the Lord] who satisfies your desires with good things so that your youth is renewed like the eagle's" (v. 5)*

Are you on the lookout for God every day? David was. A paraphrase of Psalm 103:5 could read, "Note to self, David: God satisfies all your desires with good things so that your life has exciting purpose. Pay attention!"

We build our legacy with stories of what God has done in our lives. But in order to build those stories we need a mindset that seeks to catch God in the act of working in our lives and the lives of those we interact with every day. David writes, "One thing I ask from the LORD, this only do I seek: that I may dwell in the house of the LORD all the days of my life, to gaze on the beauty of the LORD and to seek him in his temple" (Ps. 27:4). David put the exclamation point on this sentiment when he wrote, "Better is one day in your courts than a thousand elsewhere; I would rather be a doorkeeper in the house of my God than dwell in the tents of the wicked" (Ps. 84:10). Are you looking for God to show up? We need to post ourselves in His presence so we don't miss a thing.

The same Spirit that inspired David to pen those words lives in us. We can have that one thing mind-set too. It all starts with an expectation that God is going to show up everyday. "My soul, wait silently for God alone, for my expectation is from Him." (Ps. 62:5, NKJV)

What He Will Do – *"But from everlasting to everlasting the LORD's love is with those who fear him, and his righteousness with their children's children—with those who keep his covenant and remember to obey his precepts. The LORD has established his throne in heaven, and his kingdom rules over all" (vs. 17-19)*

We have a promise that God is faithful to keep creating remembrances of his love in our lives. His righteousness will go with those who fear him for multiple generations—"with their children's children." That's a legacy promised to those who keep His commands. This is the hope we have and the baton we pass on.

The Master Template

Remembrance was part of the Israel's legacy from the beginning. After Moses struck the rock to get water for the complaining sojourners "he called the placed Massah, and Meribah, because of the striving of the children of Israel, and because they tempted Jehovah" (Ex. 17:7, ASV). Moses wanted Israel to remember that rebellion and God's providence every time the city's name was mentioned. He was establishing a remembrance; building a monument.

Shortly after that incident the Israelites faced the Amalekites in battle. Moses, Aaron, and Hur went to the top of a hill to help Moses pray for Joshua's victory. As long as Moses held up his hands the Israelites prevailed. When his arms became heavy, Aaron and Hur held them up for him—one on each side. After Joshua led the army to victory over the Amalekites, God told Moses to "write this for a memorial in a book, and rehearse it in the ears of Joshua" (Ex. 17:14, ASV). To make sure there was no doubt, Moses also built an altar and named it "the Lord is my Banner." (Ex. 17:15)

I'll bet that by the end of forty years, Moses had a whole scrapbook brimming with stories of their journey to pass on to Joshua. God wants us to do the same: remember what He has done by recording those memories so we can share them with our circle of influence. Build your monuments.

But the remembrance prompt of all prompts is the ark of the covenant—the symbol of God's presence that went before Israel on their journey in the wilderness. Inside that ark were three symbols of remembrance that signified their entire journey: Aaron's miraculous rod, the stone tablets containing the commandments, and a gold jar of manna (Heb. 9:4). Each one had a story they were to tell as long as there was breath in their lungs.

Beware of Your Philistines

When the aging high priest Eli appointed his two sons to guard the ark, it seems his judgment was as cloudy as his failing eyesight. The wayward pair abused their position of power to indulge their appetites, in more ways than one. Forgetfulness and self-indulgence caused them to think of the ark as just another chest of stuff they had to haul around "for they were treating the Lord's offering with contempt" (1 Sam. 2:17). Contempt and self-indulgence are not a good combination. When the elders called for the sons to bring the ark to the battlefront to thwart a potential rout by the Philistines, the two scoundrels were cut down in battle along with thirty thousand Israelite foot soldiers. The Philistines also grabbed the ark and it wasn't returned until some twenty years later (1 Sam. 4:10-11).

Our "ark of remembrances" needs regular tending and care. We all have Philistines in our life that distract us from gathering and celebrating our remembrances. The stories and objects inside our ark have tremendous power to encourage the people God has put in our lives to influence. What's in your ark?

The Good, The Bad, The Ugly

God did not ask Israel to remember just the good times: the miracles of water, the manna, and Mount Horeb. He asked them to remember some bitter times as well. Growth comes in times of adversity, and some of the most powerful stories we have are of God bringing us through valleys of trouble. Sometimes those valleys are fear (crossing the Red Sea—Exodus 14), and sometimes they are the ugly head of rebellion (the bronze serpent on the pole—Numbers 21).

Our legacy is unrealistic if all we ever do is tell about the blessings we get from God. What about the troubles? How did we handle them? Do you have stories of failure that produced growth and brought you closer to God? Or stories about having to face a certain pesky life lesson again and again? Those stories are part of our legacy too and will all strengthen the faith of those around us.

A Method to the Madness

So how do we collect the stories and events to remember? The Bible is filled with inspiration. Let's take a look.

- *Naming of towns and locations* (Ex. 17:7, Gen. 32:22-31). Giving an experience a name is a great way to remember. Do you have a special place you go for a family vacation every year? Did you get baptized in a nearby lake or river? We can help a memory stand out by giving it a name related to where it took place.

- *Write a story or take a picture* (Exodus 17:14). Chronicle important events with written stories. Keep a journal. Start a scrapbook of pictures. Just make sure you don't hide it away where you can never see it. Keep it where it can be a conversation starter.

- *Build an altar or pillar* (Ex. 17:15,Gen. 28:10-22). Maybe not a real one, but you can commemorate an event with a tangible object that you can see and touch. It might be a desktop picture you frame from a special event. Or it might be a rock you pick up from a special event (like the flat one I found to write on).

- *Tell stories* (Ex. 18:7-11). We'll tackle how to tell a good story in chapter six.

- *Be creative: sing, draw, paint, write poetry.* Moses' sister Miriam sang a song after crossing the Red Sea (Ex. 15:1-18). Read it to get inspiration on how creative arts can create remembrances. The Bible is full of songs and poems. Just read Psalms for inspiration. Placing inspirational artifacts around your home is a visual cue to remember.

- *Traditions and celebrations:* (Luke 22:19) Traditions connected to celebrations make memorable stories. Christians today still celebrate the sacrament of communion to remember Christ's death. Do you have specific holiday traditions you celebrate every year?

One caution: sometimes when we collect mementos, we store them away. They need to live and breathe and be a part of who we are. Keep your remembrances where they can inspire a trip down memory lane.

An Elephant Never Forgets, But God Does

Even though our screw-ups are part of our legacy, we don't need to dwell on them all. We don't serve a sadistic, punitive God who loves to remind us of how pathetic we are. He picks and chooses the lessons He wants us to remember with loving care. We should do the same.

It would be a good idea for us to remember to forgive ourselves. Hebrew 8:12 says, "For I will forgive their wickedness and will remember their sins no more." We serve a God of grace. When we look back to remember, it's to remember what God has done not what we've done wrong. Grace on, guilt off.

My prayer for you: O God, may we see your works again; let our families and those you have put in our lives see your glory (Ps. 90:16). Help us to remember.

DAY ONE: DIGGER DEEPER

Pray and ask God for wisdom as you consider what stood out to you in this week's reading. Write your thoughts in your study journal. Look intently into God's Word and you will be blessed in what you do (Jas. 1:25).

1. Read Psalm 106:7. How does establishing a habit of remembrance keep us from rebelling against God?
2. Do you collect mementos of important occasions? Describe a few that come to your mind and what they represent?
3. When you receive an answer to a prayer or experience a spiritual milestone in your life, do you commemorate that event? If so, how?
4. Look again at the examples of remembrance from the Bible. Which of those appeals to you? Have you practiced any of these? If so, describe a few and what they mean to you.
5. What kinds of tangible reminders of God's work in your life do you have around your home?

6. Read Exodus 15:1-18. What imagery stands out to you? What phrases do you see repeated in this song? Why do you think those elements are important?

DAY TWO: LEGACY BUILDING BLOCKS

BUILDING MONUMENTS – MAKING MEMORIES

Truth Fact: A woman finishing well compiles mementos and stories of what God is doing in her life to share with people in her circle of influence.

1. Consider one or more of these suggestions for marking special events:

   a. Do you have photo albums? Put them out in your living room in a place where you can grab them quickly. Photos are great conversation starters.

   b. Gathering photos: Commemorate special events with pictures. Most phones have great cameras. You can make prints easily by uploading pictures directly from your phone or computer to photo processing sites in Target and Wal Mart stores easily and inexpensively. You may not be a scrapbooker, but you can archive important events and save the pictures in albums. I suggest dating photos on the back.

   c. Do you have inspirational art or décor items around your house? There are so many wonderful places to pick up these remembrances. Try Hobby Lobby or Etsy. I love having visual reminders hanging in my home of God's goodness.

   d. Do you have children that visit for special occasions? How about planning a small inexpensive craft project they can take home with them to mark the occasion? Make sure they leave behind one for you.

   e. When families gather, be sure and haul out your memorabilia. I've found that laying albums and keepsakes out on a table where we are gathering draws people's curiosity and produces some wonderful walks down memory lane.

2. Consider purchasing a memory journal. These pre-made diaries have a series of questions for you to answer about important events in your life that you can turn into stories to pass on to family members and friends. Their "question prompts" make it easy to assemble a wealth of memories. Amazon has quite a few. Just search "memory journals."

DAY THREE: FIRST THINGS FIRST
ADDING REMEMBERING TO YOUR DAILY PRAYER TIME

Remembering what God has done is part of the fourth "W" in First Things First: **waiting on God**. We'll look at the practice of prayer in part two of the book but I wanted to introduce the subject of remembrance as a regular part of our prayer routine in this chapter.

1. If you have prayer lists, consider recording the dates of answered prayers. Routinely revisiting these memories builds your faith and gives you a stockpile of stories you can recall of how God is working in your life (2 Cor. 1:4). Consider including "remembering" as a regular part of your prayer time.

2. In addition to documenting prayer requests in your journal, considering adding a page of times when God intervened in your life in ways you were not expecting. I have a journal page called "Remember what God has done," and it includes dated items such as:
   a. Son-in-law found a new job where he didn't have to commute.
   b. Successful surgery of a family member.
   c. Saved from serious injury in fall from a ladder.
   d. Successful gall bladder surgery.
   e. Able to help a favorite nonprofit continue for another year with a timely donation with money my dad left me after his death.
   f. A double rainbow one morning during a season of discouragement.

3. Some of these items are answered prayer requests that need remembering and some of them are random events where God intervened in a way I wasn't expecting. It isn't the size or magnitude of the event that's important; it's remembering the cumulative ways God has shown up in your life. Start documenting your remembrances in your study journal.

Start your list by writing down one event in the last week where you know God intervened in a supernatural way. If you cannot think of anything, put a prayer request on your list for God to open the eyes of your heart so you can see Him showing up in your life. Remember, it doesn't have to be a mountain-moving miracle, but it may be. Keep your spiritual eyes and ears open.

CHAPTER SIX

STORYTELLING
MAKING GOD'S FAITHFUNESS KNOWN

"If history were taught in the form of stories,
it would never be forgotten."

– Rudyard Kipling

"I will open my mouth with a parable; I will utter hidden things, things from of old—things we have heard and known, things our ancestors have told us. We will not hide them from their descendants; we will tell the next generation the praiseworthy deeds of the LORD, his power, and the wonders he has done."

—Psalm 78: 2-4

The History of Storytelling

When I was a junior in high school, U.S. history was a required subject. I hated it. My teacher was a former government statistician. Can you imagine what our classes were like? Lectures overflowing with dates, places, and names and then tests asking us to pour it all back like drain water into a storm sewer. I couldn't imagine a duller class … ever.

If only my teacher would have borrowed a few pointers from David, Asaph, and Moses—my favorite storytellers in the Bible. The Bible is a grand narrative, a collection of stories that includes historic events, miraculous tales of seas parting, whales spitting people out, wandering desert journeys, sugary wafers appearing mystically on the ground with morning dew, massive walls tumbling down at the shout of a crowd, angel visitations, the dead coming to life, giants falling dead at the hand of a young boy with a slingshot, and even a virgin birth. All these stories are woven into a picturesque tapestry of God's amazing grace and redemption in Jesus Christ. The Bible *is* the greatest story ever told.

Six Truths from the Master Storytellers

In the Psalms, David promises to carry on the tradition of telling the stories of God's faithfulness that were passed on to him:

> One generation commends your works to another; they tell of your mighty acts. They speak of the glorious splendor of your majesty—and I *will meditate* on your wonderful works. They tell of the power of your awesome works—and I *will proclaim* your great deeds. (Ps. 145:4-6, emphasis added)

To pass on the stories of what God has done in our lives, we need to do two things: keep our memories active (meditate) and learn how to tell a good story (proclaim).

In another psalm David's worship leader and scribe, Asaph, gives us six truths about stories we should be gathering, remembering, and telling:

> I will open my mouth with a parable; I will utter things, things from of old—things we have heard and known, things our ancestors have told us. We will not hide them from their descendants; we will tell the next generation the praiseworthy deeds of the Lord, his power, and the wonders he has done. He decreed statutes for Jacob and established the law in Israel, which he commanded our ancestors to teach their children, so the next generation would know them, even the children yet to be born, and they in turn would tell their children. Then they would put their trust in God and would not forget his deeds but would keep his commands. They would not be like their ancestors a stubborn and rebellious generation, whose hearts were not loyal to God, whose spirits were not faithful to him. (Ps. 78:2-8)

1. *We are commanded to tell stories (v. 2-3).* Storytelling, whether to family, friends, or strangers, is not just about our stories. Passing on a legacy means passing on stories you've heard from others as well.
2. *Stories of God showing up in our lives belong to everyone* (v.4). We never know how, when, or where God might use us in someone's life to convey His faithfulness. We must always be listening and be willing to share how God shows up in our lives. Don't hide the goodness of God.
3. *Learn how to tell parables (v.5).* A parable is a story with a moral lesson that illustrates God's truth. A story of obedience or disobedience is infinitely more powerful than just reciting the laws of God. It's one thing to memorize the ten commandments and another thing to illustrate them from our own lives.
4. *Encourage others to tell their own stories (v.6).* We can spark this fire by building storytelling into our friend and family gatherings. Prod people to share by giving the group a topic or recalling a memorable event and asking for their take.
5. *Storytelling increases faith and trust in God (v.7).* If we forget what God has done, we will be starting our faith over every time there is trouble on the horizon. Stories that are embedded in our hearts can become our default help when dark clouds start to gather. Remind yourself of what God has already done.
6. *Storytelling can help us avoid rebellion and sin.* Forgetting what God has done is an invitation to turn away. Also, stories of rebellion can help cement God's holiness and justice in the hearts of the hearers (v.8).

When Bad Things Happen: Remember

When it comes to telling stories, we all want to expound the wonderful things God has done in our lives, right? But what about the trials? The trouble? The rebellion? Putting our trouble in the proper perspective can give us courage and remind us that God is a loyal deliverer. People around us will draw strength from our "struggle stories."

When we are faced with difficulty, we can turn to stories about how God showed up in similar impossible situations. When King Saul told David he was no match for Goliath, David told Saul a story:

> Your servant has been keeping his father's sheep. When a lion or a bear came and carried off a sheep from the flock, I went after it, stuck it and rescued the sheep from its mouth. When it turned on me, I seized it by its hair, struck it and killed it.…. The LORD who rescued me from the paw of the lion and paw of the bear will recue me from the hand of this Philistine. (1 Sam. 17:34-37)

After the story, Saul said to David, "Go, and the Lord be with you." David had the courage to tackle Goliath because he remembered how God had delivered him before. The times we are fearful, worried, hurt, or discouraged and God brought us through–those are the stories we need to tell as well.

The Elements of a Good Story

Storytelling is an art form. But like all art, there is a pattern to making it more powerful. All good oral and written stories have these elements:

1. *Setting:* Where did it happen? Make your listeners feel like they are there with you. What was the mood? Set up the story. What were the stakes? What did you have to gain or lose? Can you connect sensory elements to the setting? Was it dark? Loud? Quiet? Raining? Summer? What were the sounds you heard?
2. *Characters:* There are usually two characters in every story: the protagonist, or main character, and the antagonist who opposes the protagonist. Their roles should be clear in your story.
3. *Plot*: This is the sequence of events that connect your listeners to the ultimate goal of the protagonist. What is the main character trying to accomplish?
4. *Conflict*: An element that drives the story. This is where many storytellers fail. A recitation of events will not be as impactful as describing the events of the conflict. For instance, look at these two accounts of the same event:

a. "We got caught in a storm on the way home."

b. "We were in a hurry to get home for the weekend. Like most college kids, we hit the road just before dark. Suddenly we hit an unexpected snowstorm so thick we could barely see the road ahead of us. We decided to stop at an all-night truck stop. The owners were gracious enough to let us nap in a booth until the storm died down. The next morning, after some hot coffee and a prayer for safety, we hit the road."

Which of these two accounts are going to pull the listener in and engage their senses and emotions?

5. *Theme*: This is the lesson entwined in the story and is sometimes called the resolution.

Let's see how these elements might work in one of the most widely told stories in the Bible—the Israelites crossing the Red Sea in Exodus 14.

* *Setting*: The Israelites are poised on the edge of the Red Sea waiting for instructions to move. They turned and saw all Pharaoh's chariots and horsemen coming after them. They cried to the Lord and to Moses. They were angry and accused Moses of bring them out to the desert to die.

- *Characters*: This story has two main characters: Moses and Pharaoh.
- *Plot*: Moses is trying to get the Israelites across the Red Sea, away from the Egyptians. He is following God's commands so that the Egyptians will be destroyed, and all the nations will know that He is the God of Israel.
- *Conflict*: These are the events of the story that move the action forward.
  i. The angel of the Lord and the pillar of cloud move to the back of the Israelite encampment coming between them and the Egyptians.

  ii. Moses stretched out his staff over the sea and all night long the wind drove back the sea and turned into dry land with a wall of water on the right and left.

iii. All Pharoah's horses, chariots, and horsemen pursued them into the sea. God threw the Egyptians into confusion and jammed the wheels of their chariots. They were terrified.

iv. At daybreak Moses stretched out his hand again and the entire army was swallowed up in the sea. No one survived.

- *Theme*: "And when the Israelites saw the mighty hand of the LORD displayed against the Egyptians, the people feared the LORD and put their trust in him and in Moses his servant (Ex. 14:31).

All your personal stories won't be this elaborate, but these are the pieces that make emotional connections with listeners and readers.

Chronicling the Story

Stories can take many forms. Telling an oral narrative is one way to pass on a story. You can also tell a story with pictures you've taken, or with a video. You may enjoy writing out your stories. In Exodus 15, Moses' sister Miriam chronicles crossing the Red Sea with a song and community celebration. Her song has some classic poetic devices including repetition which is used to emphasize a feeling, create a rhythm, or highlight a message.

In this Miriam's song (vv. 1-21), the theme or moral of the story is repeated like the chorus in a song: "I will sing to the Lord, for he is highly exalted. Both horse and driver he has hurled into the sea" (vv.1, 4, 19, 21). At the end of her song, Miriam picked up a tambourine and all the women followed her, with tambourines and dancing (v. 20). This story became a community celebration and a cornerstone in the history of the Israelites. Do you have any cornerstone stories in your family or with your friends?

It's Never Too Late to Start Telling Your Stories

Now I'm not suggesting you pick up a tambourine at your next family celebration and dance around the living room. But there are special celebrations for special events. Make sure you are building these into your legacy life. Don't be discouraged if your family and friends look at you like you're crazy when you start building a stash of stories that recount the important events in your life. Include them in the telling. Ask for their recollections. Make stories a part of your life. Rather than telling people what they should do, try telling them what you've been through.

"Give praise to the LORD, proclaim his name; make known among the nations what he has done, and proclaim that his name is exalted. Sing to the LORD, for he has done glorious things; let this be known to all the world" (Is. 12:4-5).

My prayer for you: Help us to remember what you have done, God. Teach us to chronicle the ways you show up in our lives, share our stories with others, and give praise to Your glorious name for what you've done.

DAY ONE: DIGGING DEEPER

Pray and ask God for wisdom as you consider what stood out to you in this week's reading. Write your thoughts in your study journal. Look intently into God's Word, and you will be blessed in what you do (James 1:25).

1. Read Psalm 78:1-8. What kinds of stories is the psalmist encouraging us to retell? Who should we be telling our stories to?
2. Read 2 Chronicles 16:7-9. What were the consequences to Asa's reign because of his forgetfulness?
3. Review the six truths from master storytellers of the Bible. Is there one that resonates with you more than the others? Are there any here you need to put on your prayer list?
4. Do you have a personal stash of stories like David's in 1 Samuel 17:34-37 you can tell yourself when faced with trouble? Write out one or two in your journal.
5. Do you find it hard to identify the elements of conflict when you're telling a story? How many are too many? How few are not

enough? Read the Red Sea crossing story in Exodus 14 again. Are there any elements in this list you would take out to shorten the story? Is there anything you might have included to make the story more engaging?

6. Read the account of Mary being visited by an angel in Luke 1:26-38. Make note of how the five elements of story are revealed in this account.

7. Read Matthew 1:18-23. How is this account of the virgin birth different from the version in Luke?

DAY TWO: LEGACY BUILDING BLOCKS
YOUR MOST AMAZING STORY

Truth Fact: A woman finishing well knows her personal story well and courageously tells it to show the goodness and glory of God.

Your most amazing story is the account of how God redeemed you and set you free from the power of sin and death. This is a story you should be able to tell any place, any time, when the Spirit of God opens an appropriate door. The story of how God saved you should be the most powerful chapter in your storybook. If you've never taken time to commit it to heart, let's do it.

1. Write down your reflections to the questions in each section. They will help you put a narrative together.
   - *Setting*: what are the details of the event? If you were saved as a child and don't know any of the details, let's start with the account of when your redemption became a personal lightning rod. Describe the scene. What was the mood? What time of year? Where were you? Alone or with others? What was going on in your life at the time?
   - *Characters*: You and God mainly. If you were led to Christ by a preacher, evangelist, or friend, they would be secondary characters.
   - Plot: What is the driving conflict that brought you to that point? Do you remember why you decided to trust in Christ at that time?

- *Conflict*: Were there a series of events surrounding your conversion that moved your personal story to a different trajectory?
- *Resolution*: How did that experience change your life? Many times people who are delivered from dark life experiences shed friends, family, or situations after they are saved. Always be able to tell your story without graphic, gory details. If you think you are treading close to that edge, enlist a trusted friend to help.

4. *Write out your story*. Practice reading it out loud. Be sure you have different versions for different scenarios: short, medium, full-length, for unsaved friends and family, for saved friends and family, for strangers who ask. One tip: make sure your story of salvation is user-friendly for someone who has never read the Bible. Avoid "Christian" phrases like *saved, personal savior, sanctification, redeemed*, etc. Your Christian friends will get it; your unsaved friends and family will not.

5. Work on your personal redemption story over the next months. Tell it to yourself at least once a week. Enlist a friend to help you make it "friendly" to people who don't you well and especially people who don't know the Bible. Everyone isn't an evangelist— you're not rehearsing to lead people to Christ necessarily. This story is part of your legacy.

DAY THREE: FIRST THINGS FIRST
REMEMBERING YOUR STORIES

1. In chapter five I encouraged you to start building a remembrance list with your prayer requests. How's that list coming? If you're having trouble finding things to write, ask God to help you be on the lookout for Him in your everyday.

2. If you do have a list started, take one item off that list that might make a good story and, using the five elements of story, write out a brief account of that event. You may not be able to use all five elements, but do the best you can.
   - Start out by jotting down the elements in a list.

- Next, read over the list a few times to get a feel for the movement of the story.
- Next, write out an account using conversational language.
- Read it aloud. Does the story move forward comfortably?
- Rehearse the story a few times this week until you can tell it informally.

PART TWO

TRAINING FOR THE RACE
BUILDING LEGACY HABITS

"There are no shortcuts to any place worth going."

—Beverly Sills, opera singer

"Do you not know that in a race all the runners run, but only one gets the prize? Run in such a way as to get the prize. Everyone who competes in the games goes into strict training. They do it to get a crown that will not last, *but we do it to get a crown that will last forever."*

—1 Corinthians 9:24-25, emphasis added

Running the Marathon

Unless you're The Flash, your body isn't wired to run a marathon on a whim. Training for a marathon is hard methodical work that requires a detailed practice plan that can include twenty weeks of running forty to fifty miles a week. That's if you're already in good shape.

In the same way, building a legacy lifestyle requires consistent training. The habits you establish will keep you "in shape" to run your race to the finish. Remember those tips from marathoner Nick Arciniaga in the introduction? Those are the tools he uses to run his best marathon. In this part of the study, we're going to look at the basic training tools we need to run our best race and build a legacy that lasts for generations.

The Right Stuff

There are four legacy habits you need to build your legacy and finish well: (1) personal Bible study, (2) prayer, (3) personal worship, and (4) one-anothering (friendship and fellowship). I'm using the qualifier "personal" in two of these to remind you that listening to a message on Sunday or singing worship songs in church are corporate habits—group experiences. To live a legacy life you'll need to spend *personal* time with God as well. Both corporate and personal disciplines are ideal, but I find that people often exclude personal habits thinking that their corporate experience is enough. It is not.

These legacy habits will help you firmly establish the new spiritual DNA you formed in part one of the study. Here is where the rubber meets the road. You have the scriptural foundation. Now you need to build your legacy life on that foundation. You need the right tools.

The Distraction of Busyness

Life is distracting. When we get busy, we sometimes let personal time with God fall to the wayside. If we ignore our personal connection with God, pretty soon that neglected leak under the sink becomes a couple inches of water on the floor. Instead of fixing the leak, we just pull on our rain boots and slosh around. After all, we're busy with other things. We'll fix it later. At least we're not getting wet.

Spiritual habits benefit us in two ways:

1. The deeper connection with God draws us into a more extended relationship with Him. His regular presence starts to feel like a second skin.
2. That deeper connection also keeps the eyes of our heart wide open to the activity of then enemy in our lives (Eph. 1:18).

In order to maintain that kind of spiritual depth and perseverance, long-distance training is required. This part of the study has you covered.

CHAPTER SEVEN

GOD'S TRAINING MANUAL
PERSONAL BIBLE STUDY

The law of the LORD is perfect, refreshing the soul. The statutes of the LORD are trustworthy, making wise the simple. The precepts of the LORD are right, giving joy to the heart. The commands of the LORD are radiant, giving light to the eyes…. They are more precious than gold, than much pure gold; they are sweeter than honey…. By them your servant is warned; in keeping them there is great reward.

—Psalm 19:7-11

A Tale of Two Carpenters

These words I speak to you are not incidental additions to your life, homeowner improvements to your standard of living. They are foundational words, words to build a life on. If you work these words into your life, you are like a smart carpenter who built his house on a solid rock. Rain poured down, the river flooded, a tornado hit—but nothing moved that house. It was fixed to the rock. But if you just use my words in Bible studies and don't work them into your life, you are like a stupid carpenter who built his house on the sandy beach. When a storm rolled in and the waves came up, it collapsed like a house of cards. (Matt. 7:24-27, MSG)

In Matthew 7 we see two carpenters: one who chose wisely and one who did not. There is a lot that goes into building a house: planning, gathering materials, gathering tools, and choosing a location. But everything starts with the foundation. If the foundation is bad, you'll have a lifetime of tedious work on your hands just to hold everything together.

So the question becomes, what spiritual foundation are you building on? If your life falls apart like a house of cards when the storms of trouble come, it may be you are living on sand. Is it time to move your house to a different location? A legacy of faith is built on solid rock. It is a life that is committed to following God, not just checking a weekend box and going merrily on our way.

Personal Bible study is nonnegotiable. It is the solid foundation for finishing well. And even though there is some value in a cursory reading of the Scriptures, God's Word is meant to travel from our mind to our heart and permeate every deed and decision we make throughout our day. It is an intentional process; a foundation that anchors our busy lives on an immovable rock. It is what sustains us when times are good and when times are bad.

Start with the Who

The Bible is a book about God, not a book about us. On every page, in every verse, God clearly reveals to us who He is. Yes, I see some of you rolling your eyes. Not a revelation? But ask yourself if that is really how you *study* the Bible. Many of us read the Bible to answer the questions, "who am I?" and "what should I do?" We are on the hunt for information about ourselves. It's true that God is interested in those things, but only as they come to us through the filter of who He is.

In Jen Wilkin's book *Women of the Word*, she tells the story of Moses confronting God in the burning bush. He asks a series of questions about God's proposed assignment that focused completely on his own inabilities and not on who God is. His focus was off.

When we make the Bible a book about us we need to reconsider our approach. Wilkin reminds us that unless we are looking at who we are and what we should be doing through the lens of God, our transformation is incomplete. When everything we are looking for in the Bible comes through God's eyes we see the complete picture in light of our humanity. Wilkin says, "there can be no true knowledge of self apart from the knowledge of God."

Follow with the Why

Psalm 119, the longest chapter in the Bible, is a beautiful poetic picture of the value of God's Word. The psalm is divided into twenty-two stanzas, one for each letter of the Greek alphabet, extolling the benefits of infusing God's Word into our lives. Here are just a few:

- Keeps us on the path to purity which produces delight (vv. 9-16).
- Great peace and stability for those who love it (v. 165).
- Keeps us from being put to shame (vv. 5-6).
- Gives joy to our hearts (v. 111).
- Helps us make important decisions (v. 105).
- Gives us comfort in suffering (vv. 50).
- Becomes a joyful heritage for us to pass on (vs. 111-112).

Additional benefits from other places in God's Word:

- Give us life (Pro. 3:2).
- Gives us wisdom about what to pray (John 15:7).
- Holding to it and abiding in it gives us freedom (John 8:32).

We are family members with benefits.

Separate the Meat from the Bone

I am a fan of the TV show *Chopped* on the Food Network. Every week a group of four chefs compete with the assignment of making enticing dishes out of a basket of mismatched ingredients such as quail, dandelion greens, dried currants, and hot-sauce-flavored candy canes. Now what would you make with that?

One of the most challenging *Chopped* ingredients is a slab of meat that needs to be butchered. In the short amount of time given to compose each dish, chefs who excel in knife skills usually get higher marks. They skillfully and quickly divide every piece of meat into two piles: the prime cuts of meat and the scrap pile.

Like those skilled chefs, God's Word has the power to separate our innermost thoughts and intentions so that we can discern what is God and what belongs in the scrap pile.

For the word of God is alive and active. Sharper than any double-edged sword, it penetrates even to dividing soul and spirit, joints and marrow; it judges the thoughts and attitudes of the heart. (Heb. 4:12)

As our Bible study becomes more about connecting with the living God and less about ticking off a box, we will see it take an active part in our lives. The Holy Spirit begins separating and slicing away the pieces of our lives that reveal our selfish intentions and our deepest fears.

The Bible can help us deal with the gray areas in our lives. Scripture helps us recognize right and wrong. When we learn to correctly handle the word of truth (2 Tim. 2:15), we will be able to recognize sin for what it is: a decision that separates us from our loving Father.

In 2017, research firm The Barna Group reported that 58 percent of Americans surveyed thought the Bible was the inspired Word of God with no errors. That same report indicated that only 20 percent engage with the Bible more than four times a week.[1] That is a wide disconnect between believing the Bible is truth and wanting to actually know that truth. But the Bible is not just a truth; it is *the* truth.

Listen and Do

God's Word can penetrate every part of our lives but only if we understand the connection between listen and do. James connects the dots:

Do not merely listen to the word, and so deceive yourselves. Do what it says. Anyone who listens to the word but does not do what it says is like someone who looks at their face in a mirror and, after looking at himself, goes away and immediately forgets what he looks like. But whoever looks intently into the perfect law that gives freedom, and continues in it—not forgetting what they have heard, but doing it—they will be blessed in what they do. (James 1:22-25)

James says if we just read the Bible, we are deceiving ourselves. That's a harsh warning. Focusing in on verse 25, James give us four instructions for studying and applying God's word:

1. *Look intently.* The Greek word for look intently in this verse means to stoop down to look at something more closely, to look for proof. It was also used in John 20:5 when Peter raced to the tomb and looked intently inside for evidence that Jesus was there. Our study of the Bible, however short or long, must be an intentional examination not a casual glance.

2. *Continue to do this.* Bible study needs to be a regular habit. If you're out of the habit, no problem. Start today. If you miss a couple days, start again. God's desire to spend time with you never changes.

3. *Not forgetting what you have heard.* Remembering is not an accident; it is a practice. As my Grandma used to say when I whined about practicing the piano, "practice makes perfect."

4. *But doing it.* This is where the real life change happens. This is where the Scripture moves from our mind to our heart and then influences our will—all by the grace of God. This is where become doers of the Word.

Be One of the 20 Percent

Start by making it your goal to be part of the 20 percent that the Barna report said actively engage with the Bible at least four times a week. Do you have a method for getting that Scripture from the page into your life? I call this interactive Bible study, and I'll give you a formula. One of the simplest, yet most effective ways to study your Bible is using the acronym SOAP:

S = Scripture
O = Observation
A = Application
P = Prayer

In our First Things First lesson in this chapter, we are going to set up a Bible study time each morning that fits your schedule, your resources, and your personal needs. We will use the SOAP method to help you get the most from your time. Let's take a quick look at what each of these pieces looks like:

- Scripture: In your journal, write the Scripture reference you'll be studying. It might be from a reading plan, a daily devotional, a Bible study, or a particular passage you're interested in. If you're just beginning, I recommend you start with a devotional reading plan like one of the apps in chapter four on page XX. I've included a short list of paperback devotionals in the First Things First section of this chapter for those of you that prefer a hard copy.
- Observation: What jumps out at you in this passage? Who is talking? Who is the audience? What comes right before and after the passage you are reading? If you are using a devotional or reading plan, there may be a reading that comments on the passage. If you've read this passage before, did you see anything new?
- Application: How does this apply to you? This is where the verses become personal. Listen. Is the Holy Spirit drawing your mind to a particular change or action you need to take? Is there a truth that you can take away to begin working into your life?
- Prayer: Is there a way you can personalize a prayer from this Scripture? Ask God to give you wisdom about this passage and bring it to your mind throughout the day. If there is sin to confess, do it now. If there is something to work into your life today, ask God to hold you accountable. Thank Him.

The First Things First morning routine can take as little as ten minutes—enough time to get your day focused on God but not so long that it would deter you from building the habit daily. But one promise I did not make is that you would be satisfied with just ten minutes. I believe that once you start meeting with God regularly, you'll want more. And if you're already at ten minutes, maybe you'll want to try for fifteen or twenty. It's not about the time; it's about the quality of connection.

Those who love your instructions have great peace and do not stumble. I long for your rescue, LORD, so I have obeyed your commands. I have obeyed your laws, for I love them very much. Yes, I obey your commandments and laws because you know everything I do. (Ps. 119:165-168, NLT)

My prayer for you: O God, help us to love your Word more every day. May we never be satisfied with just reading your words. Make them come to life in our lives. Open our eyes that we may see wonderful things in your Word.

DAY ONE: DIGGING DEEPER

Pray and ask God for wisdom as you consider what stood out to you in this week's reading. Write your thoughts in your study journal. Look intently into God's Word, and you will be blessed in what you do (James 1:25).

1. Read 1 Corinthians 3:10-17. What is the importance of what we build on a foundation? Why do we need to be "careful how we build?"
2. Psalm 119 is filled with the benefits of God's Word. Besides the ones I listed earlier, write down a few that you stand out to you as you read through the psalm.
3. Read James 1:22-25. How do you think we deceive ourselves if we just read the Bible without personal application?
4. Which of the four instructions in James 1:25 is the strongest in your life right now? Which is the weakest?
5. How does the SOAP Bible study method help us "rightly divide the word of truth?"
6. Which part of the SOAP acronym seems the most challenging to you? Why?

DAY TWO: LEGACY BUILDING BLOCKS
INTERACTIVE BIBLE STUDY

Truth Fact: A woman finishing well learns how to use her sword of truth with everyday practice.

The great thing about using the SOAP method for studying the Bible is that it can become a springboard for a deeper level of study. It teaches you the basic elements of interactive study. As your life with God grows, chances are your interaction with the Bible will grow as well.

1. Let's look at an example of what SOAP might look like studying Ephesians 3:20-21. I read through the passage first. Then I went back and answered all the bolded questions.

    Scripture. Write the scripture reference in your journal. Read the passage.

    Observation. **What jumps out at you in this passage?** God is able. His power is working in me to accomplish His purpose. And what He is able to accomplish surpasses anything I could even think of. I need to keep in mind that God can work in me even when I don't think anything is happening. **Who is talking here?** Paul is writing to the Ephesians, a group of believers (Eph. 1:1). **What comes right before this passage?** A prayer of Paul's for the Ephesians that they would have power to be able to grasp how high and wide and long and deep God's love is. To be filled with God's full measure.

    Application. **How does this apply to me?** God can accomplish through me much more than I can accomplish on my own. As a matter of fact, the Amplified Bible here says he can do "superabundantly more than all that we dare ask or think (infinitely beyond our greatest prayer, hopes, or dreams) according to his power that is at work in us." When I am tempted to take the steering wheel of life in my own hands, I need to remember how much more God can accomplish than I can. My efforts are puny compared to His. How could I possibly trust myself more than God? Trust is the issue I need to work on here. Pray about trusting God more.

    Prayer. Close your study time with prayer. Example: "God, help me to remember that Your power to accomplish Your purpose in my life is greater than anything I can muster. Don't let me run ahead. Teach me to listen. Thank you that You love me and care for me and want to use me to accomplish Your purpose."

2. Using the introduction Scripture in this chapter, Psalm 19:7-11, to do you own SOAP study in your journal.

DAY THREE: FIRST THINGS FIRST
GETTING STARTED WITH READING PLANS

Now that you're familiar with online reading apps from chapter four, I'll get you started with a powerful, but short reading plan called *The Heartbeat of God* by Chris Baxter. This 30-day plan is housed on the YouVersion app and features 30 daily readings from the 365 in the book. You can access this on your phone or device, or on the YouVersion website at bible.com. Following is a quick start guide to get you set up on your phone or device:

1. In your Bible app click on the Plans menu found in the footer menu. Under *Find Plans,* click on the little magnifying glass (universal icon for search) and type the title of the plan or the author in the box. Search for the Heartbeat of God by Chris Baxter. It should be at the top of your search results.

2. Click through the screens to set up the plan options and you will end up on the home screen that houses all your reading plans.

3. Tomorrow, start with day one. Keep track of your reading in your journal using the SOAP method. Each devotional should probably take about ten minutes each morning to complete depending on how much you write.

4. Other devotionals: If you need a hard copy option for a morning reading plan, I recommend the following books:

   a. *Barbour Books 3-Minute Devotional Series*. This is a short devotional, usually using just one Scripture verse. You can find these on Amazon or christianbook.com. They also have a sampler reading plan on the Bible app. The Barbour devotional usually come in hardback, paperback, and electronic form.

b. *Our Daily Bread*. This is a traditional tool available online and also on the YouVersion Bible app on your computer.

c. *First5 App.* This is from Proverbs 31 Ministries. If you want a refresher on how to download this app, the instructions are in chapter 4 on page XX. I recommend searching for a plan on a topic that catches your eye.

5. Brainstorm a list of prompts or signals you can use throughout the day to think back on your morning study. Pray for wisdom to start implementing what you're learning into your life. These prompts could be mealtimes, walking the dog, drive time to or from work, loading the dishwasher, folding the laundry. Whatever tasks you have for the day, tag them with a reminder to revisit your morning devotional time.

6. Start your morning tomorrow morning with your first three *W*s: Wake-Up Call, Water, and Word. May God bless your time together as you seek to get closer to Him.

CHAPTER EIGHT

THE ONE THING
POWERFUL PERSONAL PRAYER

"I wait for the LORD, my whole being waits, and in His word I put my hope. I wait for the LORD more than watchmen wait for the morning, more than watchmen wait for the morning."

—Psalm 130:5-6

"Never stop praying."

—1 Thessalonians 5:17, NLT

Things Are About to Change

We are about to enter uncommon territory. I ask that you hold your preconceived notions of prayer loosely in your heart. I am going to challenge your traditional practice of prayer and chart a new course for serious legacy builders. Join me as we ask God:

> "Set a fire down in my soul
> That I can't contain and I can't control
> I want more of you God
> I want more of You God."
> From "Set a Fire" by Will Reagan

Copyright © 2010 United Pursuit Music (ASCAP) Capitol CMG Genesis (ASCAP)

One Thing

The story of Aladdin, the genie, and the magic lamp is a favorite folk tale for kids of all ages; even big kids like us. Who doesn't want a magical blue genie to appear who promises to grant three wishes that will change your life?

In Psalm 27, David's enemies are in hot pursuit. "Though an army besiege me, my heart will not fear; though war break out against me, even then will I be confident" (v.3). In the midst of his trouble, with plans to evade his enemies swirling around in his head, David decides to ask God for just one thing—one wish to rule them all:

> One thing I ask from the LORD, this only do I seek; that I may dwell in the house of the Lord all the days of my life, to gaze on the beauty of the LORD and to seek him in his temple. (Psalm 27:4)

David knew the one thing that would give him the edge: remain in God's presence. Brother Lawrence, seventeenth-century author of the classic *The Practice of the Presence of God*, described this as "living as if there was none but He and I in the world."

Never Stop Praying

Now before you give me an eye roll, give me the benefit of the doubt. Isn't it possible to pray without ceasing? To always be in God's presence? Paul gave us one of the biggest keys to the Christian life in these three words: "Never stop praying" (1 Thess. 5:7, NLT). It's not really doable within the traditional definition of prayer. Nobody can sit or kneel down with a prayer list all day long. That kind of prayer is an event. Paul's admonition to never stop praying is about a lifestyle, an ever-abiding presence. This kind of prayer permeates every moment of every day. Jesus called it remaining in him (John 15:4).

When we assign praying to fixed times and places, prayer ceases to go with us throughout the day. There are times and places for certain types of prayers (we'll cover that later) but remaining in prayer is 24/7. There is *nothing* that turbo boosts our relationship with God like this kind of prayer. And nobody knows this better than our enemy.

Storming the Gates

There is nothing that rattles Satan's cage more than saints storming the gates of heaven in prayer. He knows the undeniable truth that prayer breaks chains and calms the raging seas in our troubled minds. And prayer unleashes God's power in our lives, the kind of power that slams doors shut and plugs the holes where dark forces are trying to creep in to your life. Keeping us from prayer is on the top of Satan's to-do list.

Before we dig in to prayer, let's revisit the rules of spiritual battle and get a few things straight about our enemy and his armies:

- Satan is not God. He's not on an equal plane with God.
- His power doesn't even begin to scratch the surface of what God can do.
- He is not omnipresent; he can't be everywhere at once.
- He cannot read your mind.
- He is a liar, a trickster, a deceiver, a destroyer.
- His fate is already sealed.

Our enemy sees prayer as a call to battle. So should we.

Learning to Wait

Powerful prayer is about learning to wait. There are eight different Greek words used for the English word *wait* in the Bible. Here is just a sampler:

1. *Waiting with focus and passion.* "I wait for the LORD, my whole being waits, and in his word I put my hope. I wait for the Lord more than watchmen wait for the morning, more than watchmen wait for the morning" (Ps. 130:5-6). Watchmen need a keen sense of anticipation and focus. They know exactly how to spot any irregularity in their view. Can you identify the Holy Spirit's voice speaking to you? Do you know the Scriptures well enough to discern the truth? Is being in God's presence your "one thing?"

2. *Waiting in hope.* "We wait in hope for the LORD; he is our help and our shield" (Ps. 33:20). Do we believe God's love is unfailing when circumstances look otherwise? Are we determined to wait patiently knowing that He will hear us (Ps. 40:1)?

3. *Waiting confidently.* "And without faith it is impossible to please God, because anyone who comes to him must believe that he exists and that he rewards those who earnestly seek him" (Heb. 11:6). Do we trust Him? Do we believe he can keep us from evil (Matt. 6:13)?

4. *Wait patiently.* "Wait for the Lord; be strong and take heart and wait for the LORD" (Ps. 27:14). Sometimes God says, "wait." It's the four-letter word in the Bible that makes our shoulders suddenly drop. We are an impatient lot.

An attitude of waiting keeps our hearts and minds constantly prepared to hear from God. It leaves the door open for God to get our attention. The ears of our heart are listening, even as we go about our daily routine. We are, as Brother Lawrence said, practicing the presence of God.

The Four Mind-sets of Powerful Prayer

When one of the disciples asked Jesus to teach him how to pray, Jesus fashioned the most recited prayer in history. We call it the Lord's Prayer. In Matthew 6, Jesus gave us four truths of powerful prayer that are the template for approaching the Father. In this section we are using the New Living Translation:

1. *Powerful prayer is a sacred conversation.* "Our Father in heaven, may your name be kept holy. May your Kingdom come soon. May your will be done on earth as it is in heaven" (vv. 9-10). We have received an invitation to connect with the Most Holy God. Verses 1-13 are a first person conversation. Jesus is paving the way to the Father's presence with a personal conversation; He is always keeping God's holiness and sovereignty in our sight.

2. *Powerful prayer knows God is in charge of everything.* "Give us today the food we need" (v. 11). Those who come to God must believe He is who He said He is. God is sovereign: absolute, su-

preme, infinite, and boss of everything. There is no one or nothing above Him. Everything we have, we owe to Him.

3. *Powerful prayer produces a clean heart (confession and forgiveness).* "Forgive us our sins, as we have forgiven those who sin against us" (v. 12). Personal sin is a roadblock to a deeper relationship with God. But good news: He has promised to forgive our sins and give us a new start if we just ask (1 Jn. 1:9). The catch here is the "as we have forgiven." Confession of our sins and forgiveness of others must be a regular part of our personal prayer. Jesus made it crystal clear in verses 14-16 that our unforgiveness will separate us from God. We can't afford not to forgive. We are only hurting our own relationship with God. Make no mistake: forgiveness does not mean a stamp of approval or a dismissal of what others have done. I am not downplaying the difficulty of this process. I have labored on my knees many times with unforgiveness in my heart. I just desire to see you clear the path between you and God. If you need it, get help forgiving those people who have wronged you. I've noticed that forgiveness is more often a process than a one-time declaration on our part.

4. *Powerful prayer is a battleground.* "And don't let us yield to temptation, but rescue us from the evil one" (v. 13). Remember, keeping us from praying, confessing our sins, and forgiving others is Satan's top priority. Know where the chinks in your armor are. What's tripping you up? Are you pestered by fear, doubt, bitterness, discouragement, or unbelief? The enemy will try and get you to focus on things around you: your husband, your demanding boss, your mean neighbor, your aging parent, your unrelenting physical pain, your wayward children. Don't buy it for one second. It's a ploy. Stay focused on the real battle. Remember Ephesians 6:12: you're not fighting flesh and blood enemies. The real battle is in the unseen realms—against evil rulers. Live in the armor.

Types of Prayer

There are four main types of prayers we see modeled in the Bible that we should weave into our legacy building. We need to see each of these in the frame they are intended to be displayed. All prayer is not created equal. Each has a purpose.

1. *Lifestyle*: This is the "remaining in Him" prayer we've been talking about. It is a continuing conversation with God. It is the "pray without ceasing" prayer—an open door in our hearts for God be present in everything that we do. Practice God's presence (1 Thess. 5:17).

2. *United or Corporate:* When we gather together to pray, whether it's with a friend or with a congregation, we have a super power: agreement. If we are gathering in Jesus' name, He is there with us, and God will answer that prayer (Matt. 18:19-20). We can't dictate the answer or the timing, but He will answer. Jesus promised.

   What a marvelous fellowship. How many times do we gather with friends, family, or even a spouse at dinner and not use that opportunity to agree about something in prayer? Corporate prayer isn't just for Bible studies and worship services. Two or more is all it takes.

3. *Declarations of faith and Scripture prayers.* In chapter three we talked about the power of the spoken word. Building an arsenal of personal declarations based on Scripture creates a storehouse of powerful faith. Do you have special Bible verses that remind you of who you are, what God has done for you, or a milestone you've crossed with God? Some people call these life verses, but I say make them Refrigerator Verses. They help move that truth from your head to your heart to your feet. Also, borrow prayers from Scripture. Start with Paul's prayers in the New Testament.

4. *Personal daily prayer.* This is prayer closet prayer. "But when you pray, go into your room, close the door and pray to your Father, who is unseen. Then your Father, who sees what is done in secret, will reward you" (Matt. 6:6). When most of us think of praying, this is the image we see. On our knees, in our chairs, standing with uplifted hands or on the floor flat on our faces. The posture is as personal as the prayer. In this chapter's lessons we'll give you a formula for personal prayer that will give shape to this necessary daily meeting with God.

My prayer for you: Never stop praying. It is your super power.

DAY ONE: DIGGING DEEPER

Pray and ask God for wisdom as you consider what stood out to you in this week's reading. Write your thoughts in your study journal. Look intently into God's Word, and you will be blessed in what you do (James 1:25).

1. Listen to the song, "Set a Fire" by Jesus Culture in this link. There may be an ad to click through first but don't let that stop you: https://www.youtube.com/watch?v=-Jzqq4B8H2Q. This version has the lyrics. As you listen, pray that the lyrics would ignite your spirit. Listen for the Holy Spirit to magnify its meaning as it relates to prayer. After you're done listening, journal your thoughts and reflections.

2. Read 1 Thessalonians 5:17 from several different Bible versions (you can use your YouVersion app for this). Write your definition of "never stop praying" in your journal.

3. Is there anything in our list of attributes for Satan that was a surprise to you? Make an effort this week to remind yourself of what your enemy is *not*.

4. Read the following Scriptures: Ps. 130:5-6, Ps. 33:20, Heb. 11:6, Ps. 27:14. Which of these definitions of waiting in prayer is hardest for you? Why? Put it on your prayer list.

5. Read Matthew 6:14-16. What is a condition of God forgiving our sins? Is there someone that caused you or a loved one great pain? Have you forgiven them? Describe the process. Is there anyone that needs your forgiveness? Ask God to help you through the process. Enlist the help of a trusted friend to pray. Seek a counselor's help if you need it.

6. Read Matthew 4:1-11. What did Satan use to tempt Jesus in the wilderness? What sorts of events and distractions does the enemy use to distract believers from the real battle?

7. Which of the four main types of prayer do you need to incorporate more into your life and why? Are there any you are missing?

DAY TWO: LEGACY BUILDING BLOCKS
PRACTICING GOD'S PRESENCE (NEVER STOP PRAYING)

Truth Fact: A woman finishing well never stops praying.

1. Write a personalized version of 2 Timothy 1:7 on an index card. This is your Refrigerator Verse for the week.
2. Prompts are a great way to help you cultivate the constant presence of God. They will remind you that God is always with you. Consider trying these:
   a. Conclude your First Things First morning time with a prayer of continued presence such as this:

   > O God, it's time to start my day and apply my energy to outward things. I ask you to grant me grace and mercy to stay in your presence throughout my day. Go with me and may the words of my mouth and the meditations of my heart be pleasing in your sight.

   b. Trying setting your phone alarm to chime on the hour. Use that signal to check in with God. Ask Him to heighten your awareness of His presence with you as you go throughout your day. Thank him that he is always with you.
   c. Consider carrying a short list of faith declarations with you this week on an index card (or a note on your phone) to pull out when your phone chimes on the hour.
   d. Every time you eat throughout the day, thank God for your daily bread.
   e. Before you go to bed at night, thank God for His presence with you throughout the day.
   f. If you meet a Christian friend during the day, ask them if they can take a moment to agree with you in prayer.
   g. When you're driving, use every red light as an opportunity to pray for your circle of influence.

h. Before you walk in the grocery store, coffee shop, or work, ask God to show you someone to encourage. Watch and listen for an opportunity.

i. See something beautiful in nature? Thank God for His creative touch and for reminding you of His power.

j. Consider playing Christian worship music when you are in your car.

k. Use your drive time to pray for your communities of influence.

These prompts are meant to give you more ideas on how you can start cultivating a heart that never stops praying. Use your imagination. The more you practice, the stronger the habit will become.

DAY THREE: FIRST THINGS FIRST
THE FOURTH "W" – WAIT IN PRAYER

Wait in prayer is the fourth *W* in our First Things First morning routine. We are going back to the Lord's prayer in Matthew 6:9-13 for a formula you can use to get started. Using the acronym P.R.A.Y., we'll incorporate four ingredients into our prayer recipe: praise, repent, ask, and yield.

Praise: Start your prayer time with a period of listening quietly, yielding to God's holiness. And lifting up his name in praise (v. 9). Come confidently, asking for grace and mercy (Heb. 4:16).

Repent, confess, and forgive (vv. 12-13). Clear every obstruction in the pathway between you and God. Thank God for His faithfulness in forgiving your sins (1 John 1:9). Ask God to protect you from evil and empower you to live in the armor (Eph. 6:11)

Ask: Present to God your needs and the needs of others (v. 11). Listen to His Spirit to lead you. God actually knows your needs before you even open your mouth.

Yield: Acknowledge God's will is always the best answer (vv.10, 13) Leave the answer, the timing, and the prayers with God. Be thankful to be able to leave your requests with God (Phil. 4:6). It is a peace protector. Conclude with a time of listening and yielding to God's presence. This is tough if you're not used to it, but allow time to be still.

1. If you haven't started a list of prayer requests in your journal, find a blank page and start. Transfer the ingredients of the P.R.A.Y. acronym and corresponding Scriptures to the top of that page as a reminder.
2. I suggest two "portions" of asking for personal requests. First, pray for yourself. Pray to be able to focus on the real battles going on. Name them if you can. Bring your needs before God. Pray for wisdom and understanding (Prov. 2). In addition to your personal requests, pray for the needs of others. Start with your circle of influence. What prayer requests have been sent your way? Keep track of them with dates and date the answers when they come.
3. Before you leave your prayer time each morning, ask for God's continued presence (see Day Two's lesson). Know that God is going with you. If something comes to mind to pray about during the day, shoot an express prayer to God thanking Him for the opportunity to pray for that specific person or event.
4. If you are looking for some inspired prayers to get started, here is a list of Paul's prayers you can personalize and pray. I recommend looking each one up and writing it in your prayer journal as a bonus assignment.
    a. Eph. 3:16-19
    b. Eph. 1:17-19
    c. Rom. 15:13
    d. Php. 1:9
    e. Heb. 13:20-21
    f. Col. 1:9-12
    g. 2 Thess. 1:11

I know that some of you reading this feel pulled to a ministry of intercessory prayer (prayer warrior). If that's not you, it's okay. I believe that is a gift and not something every believer is drawn to. Remember what Jesus said in Matthew 6:6-8: it isn't the quantity of time you spend in prayer, but the quality. Just be sure you are listening and responding. As this time in prayer becomes a habit, you'll gain more confidence in the method and time frame.

CHAPTER NINE

TRUE WORSHIP
BUILDING A LIFESTYLE HABIT

"But a time is coming and is already here when the true worshipers will worship the Father in spirit [from the heart, the inner self] and in truth; for the Father seeks such people to be His worshipers. God is spirit [the Source of life, yet invisible to mankind], and those who worship Him must worship in spirit and truth."

—John 4:23-24, AMP

"It is good to praise the LORD and make music to your name, O Most High, proclaiming your love in the morning and your faithfulness at night."

—Psalm 92:1-2

More Than A Song

When you picture worship, do you see an image of singing with others in church? True worship is a lifestyle, a posture of reverence in everything we do that emanates from our heart (John 4:23-24). Worship is about more than music. God is seeking true worshipers. Maybe it's time to respond to the call and expand our definition of what true worship is.

In Psalm 95, the writer opens with a call to sing for joy, shout aloud, extol God with music, and tell of His marvelous works (vv. 1-5). But the word *worship* does not show up until verse six: "Come, let us bow down in worship, let us kneel before the LORD our Maker." The Hebrew word for worship here is *shachah*, which means to bow down or fall flat. True worship starts with a submitted heart.

In John 4, Jesus had a lengthy conversation with a Samaritan woman that started when he asked her for a drink of water. After she pointed out she not supposed to talk with him, he dove right in anyway. When the conversation got a little uncomfortable—"the fact is, you have had five husbands, and the man you now have is not your husband" (v. 18)—a light bulb went off in her head. This guy is a prophet.

Turning the conversation toward religious differences, she wanted to know if it was okay to worship on the local mountain, as their custom dictated. Jesus then explained that place is not what worship is all about:

> You Samaritans worship what you do not know; we worship what we do know, for salvation is from the Jews. Yet a time is coming and has now come when the true worshipers will worship the Father in the Spirit and in truth, for they are the kind of worshipers the Father seeks. (John 4:22-23)

Your worship is not confined to a time and place (Sunday mornings). True worship is a 24/7 lifestyle displayed in a number of different ways, including music.

The Four Truths of Worship

When it comes to building a legacy of worship, we want to build our foundation on these four truths.

1. *True worship begins with the meditations of our heart and words of our mouth (Ps. 19:14).* God is seeking worshipers that have a true heart toward Him (John 4:23). The intentions of our heart are laid bare before an all-knowing God. In Isaiah 29:13 God says, "These people come near to me with their mouth and honor me with their lips, but their hearts are far from me." We can't fool God.

2. *True worship is a lifestyle, not an event (Rom. 12:1).* Our regular church attendance should enhance our worship, but it is not the sum total of it. Our "true and proper worship" is the sacrifice of a

life dedicated to serving God's purpose. That kind of worship is "holy and pleasing to God."

3. *All creation is designed to worship God (Ps. 150).* In the closing psalm we see the inclusive scope of true worship as God meant it to be. God is to be worshipped everywhere (v. 1). He is to be worshipped with singing, dancing, and the playing of instruments (vv. 3-5). And He will be worshipped by everything that has breath (v. 6). Praise the Lord!

4. *Personal worship is a vital part of every believer's life (Ps. 59:16, Ex. 29:38-39).* Early in Israel's history, the practice of morning and evening sacrifice was instituted as a reminder of the constant presence of God on Israel's behalf (Ex. 29:38-39). These sacrifices were like bookends meant to keep God's people hemmed in by a single purpose. Not just first thing in the morning (Ps. 59:16) or last thing at the end of the day but all the time.

Worship is not confined to time and place. Nor is it fenced in by convention. It can be euphoric or contemplative, loud or quiet, lying flat on the floor or sitting in a chair. It can be a cappella or with an orchestra, in your living room or in a cathedral, alone or surrounded by thousands. Whatever its form, true worship is a living sacrifice to God done in spirit and in truth.

The Five Mind-sets of Worship

Building a legacy of faith involves passing on a habit of worship—personal as well as corporate. There are five mind-sets that will help you build that legacy:

1. *Worship is our pathway out of sorrow to hope (Ps. 42).* In verses 1-3 the writer identifies his emotional condition: he is thirsting; he is sorrowful (crying day and night); he is being pestered by doubt. How often do we find ourselves here? Even though the psalmist is at a low point, he reminds himself of the powerful experience of true worship (v. 4). This is a pivotal point in his life. Recalling what God has done throughout his life (v.7) summons the deep holy roar of worship, as Chris Tomin calls it. Praising God in sorrow gives us hope (v.11). It is not easy, but the way to hope starts with remembering what God has done.

2. *Worship is a joyful expression of thanksgiving and praise to God to all generations.* Psalm 100 is a short but powerful declaration of the goodness of God for all time. It starts with a command: "shout for joy to the LORD, all the earth." We are encouraged to worship God with gladness and joyful songs. We are His people—who else should be shouting about the goodness of God in the world? Celebrate his enduring love and His faithfulness to all generations (v. 5).

I love candy corn. Every Thanksgiving growing up, those pure sugar delights would make an appearance at the dining table. My mother would carefully arrange three pieces in front of each plate on the table. Before the turkey was carved, we would take turns going around the table and telling three things we were thankful for. My mother inherited this tradition from her mother who joined us at the table in the years after my grandfather passed away. Three generations of thankfulness.

I remember fidgeting as a youngster waiting for my turn so I could gobble up the three pieces of sweet goodness. The older I got, the more I cherished the time of reflection and listening to the stories of others around the table. Some years we would close with the a cappella version of the Doxology: "Praise God from whom all blessings flow. Praise him all creatures here below. Praise him above ye heavenly hosts. Praise Father, Son, and Holy Ghost." That joyful expression of God's goodness has made its way to my own Thanksgiving table, and every year as I place the candy corn in front of each plate, I think of my mother and my grandmother and thank God for the legacy of thanksgiving they passed on to all of us.

3. *Personal worship also involves giving as a testimony of what God has done* for us. Don't worry, I'm not going to give you a lecture on tithing because giving is about more than money. Worshipful giving is about stewardship—sharing what He has given you. This goes for our time, our talents, our money, and everything God has blessed us with. Giving evokes generosity.

4. *True worship is a reciprocal relationship (James 4:8).* His deepest desire is for you to draw near to Him, so He can draw nearer to you. God has told us that when we seek Him with all our heart, we will find him. When we call on Him, he will listen (Jer. 29:12-14).

5. *Worshipping with others builds our faith (Ps. 84).* Whether you gather together in a home church or a megachurch, meeting together is part of God's plan to bless His people. In Psalm 84:10 David witnessed this blessing in a personal confession: "I would rather be a doorkeeper in the house of my God than dwell in the tents of the wicked." Quite a drop from king to doorkeeper. But David loved God's house so much he was willing to do the lowliest job just to be there: "How lovely is your dwelling place, LORD Almighty! My soul years, even faints, for the courts of the LORD; my heart and flesh cry out for the living God" (vv. 1-2). Paul admonished us not to forsake meeting together with other believers for a reason: this is where we give and receive encouragement (Heb. 10:25) while we draw near to God.

My prayer for you: O God, satisfy us in the morning with your unfailing love, that we may sing for joy and be glad all our days (Ps. 90:14). Teach us to be true worshipers. Give us a heart that would rather spend one day in your courts than a thousand anywhere else.

DAY ONE: DIGGING DEEPER

Pray and ask God for wisdom as you consider what stood out to you in this week's reading. Write your thoughts in your study journal. Look intently into God's Word, and you will be blessed in what you do (James 1:25).

1. How does Jesus' definition of true worship in John 4 differ from the practice of worship we see in churches?
2. Has this chapter challenged your traditional idea of worship? Explain.

3. When you hear the phrase "worship is a lifestyle," what does that look like to you?
4. How have you incorporated worship "prompts" into your daily routine? For instance, do you listen to Christian music, have regular times of thanking and praising God in prayer, incorporate traditions of faith into your family gathering?
5. Do you attend a church gathering on a regular basis? If so, what is the value to you personally? If not, what's holding you back?
6. Describe how you "draw near to God."

DAY TWO: LEGACY BUILDING BLOCKS
EXPLORING THE DIVERSITY OF WORSHIP

Truth Fact: A woman finishing well worships God with her whole heart, mind, soul, and strength in her personal life and with other believers.

1. Did you know that the Bible has seven specific words for praise? Each one has a unique meaning and place in lifestyle worship. Read the Scriptures following each word for praise and give your take on how each definition could play out in your life. Write your thoughts in your study journal.
   a. HALLAL: This is the main root word for praise. It means "to be clear, to praise, to shine, to boast, to show, to rave, to celebrate, to be clamorously foolish." This is where we get the word hallelujah. How do you recognize God's holiness in your life and worship?
      • Ps. 113:1-3, Ps. 150:1, Ps. 149:3, Ps. 18:3
   b. YADAH: This is a verb meaning, "to extend the hand, to throw out the hand, to lift the hands" as in worship or to worship with extended hands. It is more a word of praising God for what He has done rather than who He is. How do you express thanks and appreciation for what God has done in your life?
      • 2 Chron. 20:21, Ps. 63:1, Ps. 107:15, Jer. 33:11
   c. TOWDAH: This word comes from the same root as YADAH but literally means, "an extension of the hand in adoration or acceptance." This is a word of expectation of receiving what God has already done. What postures do you use in your personal and corporate worship?
      • Ps. 50:14, Ps. 42:4, Ps. 56:12

d. SHABACH: This word means "to shout or address in a loud tone, to command, to triumph." This word is used often to describe the physical actions of worship. How do shouting and dancing fit in to your definition of worship? How does it make you feel when others express their worship this way?
- Ps. 47:1, Ps. 145:4, Is. 12:6, Ps. 63:3

e. BARAK: This word means "to kneel down, to bless God as an act of adoration, to salute." It is a posture of humility. What postures of humility do you incorporate into your prayer and worship times? These can be physical or spiritual.
- Ps. 95:6, 1 Chron. 29:20, Ps. 34:1, Ps. 72:15

f. ZAMAR: This word means "to pluck the strings of an instrument, to sing, to praise." It is a musical word that is chiefly used to describe the use of instruments and singing. What are some of the ways you can incorporate music into your First Things First routine? Into your everyday?
- Ps. 21:13, 1 Chron. 16:9, Ps. 57:8-9

g. TEHILLAH: This word means "praise that involves the speaking or singing of words." Are you incorporating spoken Bible verses or worship lyrics into your day? What are some ways you could do that?
- Ps. 22:3, Is. 61:3, Ex. 15:11

2. The Bookends: One way to incorporate worship into your daily routine is to start a habit of setting your focus on God in the morning and ending your day with an evening declaration, similar to the morning and evening sacrifices of the Hebrews. We can model these two declarations after Ps. 92:2: "It is good to proclaim your unfailing love in the morning, your faithfulness in the evening" (NLT). God will lead me; He has brought me through every day. We already have the morning part covered in our First Things First routine: the Wake-up Call. Now we are going to add the other bookend: the evening declaration of God's faithfulness before we fall asleep. Tonight, when you climb into bed, before you turn off the light, take a moment and scan back over the day's events, thanking God for His faithfulness. Make this a daily proclamation. These are the bookends of personal worship.

DAY THREE: FIRST THING FIRST

THE FIFTH "W" – BUILDING YOUR WORSHIP PLAYLIST

Music is a powerful tool. It has the ability to intensify our focus and engage our emotions. One of God's greatest gifts, music can soothe the soul (1 Sam. 16:23), provide motivation and courage (1 Chron. 25:1), and even prepare our hearts to hear from God (2 Kings 3:15-16).

1. Worship should be an important piece of your First Things First morning routine. First, let's look at how to incorporate it into your routine using your smartphone or laptop.

    a. After you've finished your daily Bible reading and journaling, ask God to show you a song that will help you remember what you have studied. It may be an old chorus, a hymn, or a contemporary worship song. Try searching for the song in the search box on YouTube. You may get some options: a performance video or just a lyric video. I prefer the lyric videos, if they're available, because I can sing along. If you already have a worship playlist on YouTube or Spotify, you may want to glance over those lists for inspiration.

    b. Write the name of the song in your journal entry for that morning and add the song to your worship list or favorites, if it isn't already there.

    c. Play the song and listen or sing along. You may be prompted to stand, raise your hands, kneel down, or just stay seated. Respond as the Holy Spirit leads you.

2. Sometimes God will prompt us to think of a song during a prayer time as well. Repeat a-b-c above if that's a better time for you to worship. It doesn't really matter where in your morning routine you worship; just make sure that worship is a part of your morning routine. Don't forget your earbuds or ear phones if you're not the only one in the house. I have friends that also do this during a morning walk so they can get out of the house and sing with all their might. Some mornings you may find that just reciting song lyrics or an inspirational pslam is a moving worship experience. Start with these psalms: 8, 27, 42, 47, 66, 84, 95-106, 117, 121, 134-136, 146-150. I recommend experimenting with this part of your morning routine.

3. What do you listen to when you are driving? Tune your car radio to Christian music. We spend hours in our cars, and it's a perfect opportunity to keep our hearts focused. Most urban areas have Christian stations on either AM and FM radio. If you don't know if there is one in your area, search online or find one on this data base: https://www.christianradio.com/stations/. Make your drive time God time. If you have Sirius or XM radio, you have The Message.

4. If your car's radio has Bluetooth capability and you have a smartphone, you can listen to Spotify or Pandora in your car—or anywhere else you are for that matter. In Pandora's free version, you will have to listen to occasional commercials, but you can build a playlist based from searches of your favorite kind of music, such as instrumental praise or contemporary Christian. You can even build "stations" using popular Christian groups or artists such as Hillsong, Bethel Music or Chris Tomlin.

5. YouTube is also a good place to build a worship list. Most smart TVs have a dedicated YouTube app, and you can download the app to your smartphone as well. You will need a YouTube account (free with email login). Once you have an account you can mark songs you like as Favorites or build specific lists. Start by searching for your favorite Christian songs on YouTube. To learn more about how to build worship lists on YouTube, watch the video here with instructions for iPhone, Android phones, or computers: (http://bit.ly/youtubelists).

6. You now *officially* have all five parts of your First Things First routine ready to go. Tonight, before you go to bed, gather everything you need to get started the next morning. You're on your way to a new experience that will radically change your life. You'll never regret doing the work it takes to establish a morning routine. And never, I repeat, never be hard on yourself if you miss. Just start again the next day. God is a God of grace. You can do it—I'm praying for you!

7. Next time you get in your car, crank up the Christian music.

Chapter Ten

ONE-ANOTHERING
FRIENDSHIP AND FELLOWSHIP

"And let us consider how we may spur one another on toward love and good deeds, not giving up meeting together, as some are in the habit of doing, but encouraging one another and all the more as you see the Day approaching."

—Hebrews 10:24-25

"The only way to have a friend is to be one."

—Ralph Waldo Emerson

According to research published in the *New York Times* a lack of friends can kill us.[1] Social isolation breeds a number of illnesses including sleep disruption, altered immune systems, higher stress, and an increased risk of heart disease. Loneliness, a frequent companion of isolation, can disrupt our cognitive processes and lead to premature death. That's quite a case for making a few friends. But it isn't always as easy as it sounds.

Christians have a Biblical mandate to love people. We are commanded seventeen times in the New Testament to love one another. The phrase "one another" appears fifty-nine times. At the Last Supper, right after a heartbreaking confrontation with Judas, Jesus told his disciples:

> A new command I give you; Love one another. As I have loved you, so you must love one another. By this everyone will know that you are my disciples, if you love one another. (John 13:34-35)

Friendship is an earmark of the Christian faith. Introvert or extrovert, living alone or with family, working full time or retired, we are commanded to love one another. What exactly does that look like?

Five Truths of Biblical Friendship

As we explore the topic of friendship in the Bible, we'll find that loving one another is just the beginning of what we're commanded to do for each another. But one thing we all know from experience is that getting close to people can be messy, so let's open our divine user manual for some advice about the five truths of Biblical friendship.

1. *Love for Christian friends is unique.* In Romans 12:10, Paul shows us the depth of that love: "Be devoted to one another in love. Honor one another above yourselves." Paul uses the word *philadephia* here for *love*—the love of brothers. And the word *devoted* in this verse comes from the Greek word *philostorgos*, which is a cherishing, family type love; fierce and tenacious. It never lets go. "It always protects, always trusts, always hopes, always perseveres" (1 Cor. 13:7). *Oh faithful and loving God, give us this love for each other.*

2. *Christian friends sharpen one another in accountability and growth.* "As iron sharpens iron, so a friend sharpens a friend" (Prov. 27:17) is a verse we often see quoted about friendships. But what exactly does that sharpening look like?

    Many of us have seen that sleek rounded steel rod that TV chefs wield as they expertly slip their knives quickly back and forth on both sides. That tool is actually a honing steel, and it doesn't sharpen a knife. It realigns the blade after cutting has shifted its edge. The first order of business in sharpening: get your "blade" in alignment with the truth.

    Next, to sharpen a knife, you need a sharpening stone. These stones come in all grades of coarseness, like sandpaper, and the grade you need depends on how dull the edges have become. Here's what that "iron sharpening" process looks like:

a. Choose the coarseness of your stone first. How dull are the edges? Start with the coarsest stone needed to smooth the deepest pit. *When you are "sharpening" a friend, discernment is needed. We need to know our friend well enough to know what their needs are, not what we think they need.*

b. Next, you need to set the knife against the stone at the right angle for maximum sharpness. You can actually make the knife duller if the angle is too steep. *Sometimes our personality can get in the way when we are sharpening a friend, so move cautiously and pray for wisdom to discover the "angle" you need to take. And be careful of your expectations. Remember, you are sharpening in partnership with God. Listen.*

c. The stone needs some liquid, either water or oil, to carry away the particles you are smoothing off. *A good friend acts like a cleansing stream of encouragement where a sister's cares and confessions can be lifted up to God.*

d. The last step in sharpening a knife is cycling through lesser coarse stones (similar to sandpaper) to finely tune the sharp edges. *Our job in sharpening others is not just to be the heavy hand and smooth out only the deep cavities, but to bring out the best and shiniest parts of our friends—to take their hand and gently lead them back into God's presence.*

3. *Do not neglect meeting together with friends on a regular basis (Heb. 10:24-25).* These verses in Hebrews emphasize that if we don't meet together, we miss an important element we need in the Christian life: mutual encouragement. This expanded definition of meeting together shows us that it is about more than just going to church. Our weekly worship services are not the most convenient place for deep conversations. Be willing to open your home, invite people out for a quick meal or cup of coffee after church, start a Bible study or small group, reach out to that new woman in the row behind you. Being the new girl is often a scratchy, uncomfortable seat to be in. We all feel inadequate at ice breaking. Friendships all start with that first awkward conversation somewhere. Go first.

4. *Pursue close friendships with like-minded women (Ps. 1:1-3).* It is so tempting to want a seat at the popular girls' table. I think there's still a teenage girl inside each one of us wishing to be one of the

cool kids. Remember the words of the psalmist: "Oh, the joys of those who *do not* follow the advice of the wicked or stand around with sinners or join in with mockers" (v. 1). Know whether your friendships are leading you astray or leading you closer to God. It's one thing to feel a missionary tug for your neighbors or book club group and another to pursue a friendship because it feels good to be a part of the "in" crowd. Don't be fooled; when it comes to close friendships, bad company will corrupt good character (1 Cor. 15:33).

5. *Balanced friendship circles are multigenerational (Titus 2:3-5).* Paul knew that mothers and daughters have special relationships. In this passage in Titus, Paul encourages older women to befriend younger women and set an example of godliness. Younger women need our friendship, our listening ears, and our caring hearts. Many of the younger women in our churches live far away from their real mothers, and are longing for older godly women to befriend them.

What kind of friend does the Bible ask us to be? To pursue and build true friendships, we need to adopt four friendship mind-sets. They will help us build relationships we can cling to no matter what stormy sea we find ourselves in.

The Four Mind-sets of True Friendship

1. *Always live in harmony with each other (Rom. 12:16-18, Mark 9:50. Rom. 15:7).* Don't get caught up in that trap of pursuing friendships only with people that look and act like you. It may be comfortable, but Paul encourages us to associate with people at every position in life. Do not be exclusive; be inclusive. Living in harmony also means extending forgiveness and mercy when needed. If a friend hurts you, make sure it doesn't become a wedge. When your friendship starts to veer off course from unre-solved hurt, do what you need to do to right the ship. If she doesn't accept your olive branch, then you did what you could do (Rom. 12:18). Every tear in our friendship cloth cannot be mended but taking out the sewing kit should be our first step.

2. *Serve others as Christ left us an example (Gal. 5:13, Mark 10:45, Gal. 6:2).* Use your gifts, resources, and time to help out a friend in need: A meal when someone comes home from the hospital,

offering a guest room for their visiting relative, helping them pack when they are getting ready to move, offering a ride to that concert when you know they don't like to drive at night, mowing a lawn when they're sick, a phone call to check on them when you haven't seen them in a while. And don't forget the special occasions: funny birthday cards, a plate of cookies when you made an extra-large batch, a bouquet of flowers from your garden. All we have to do is keep our eyes and ears open. There will never be a shortage of opportunities if we are willing. And if this is hard for you, spend more time with a friend who is good at this. She will inspire you—and maybe even give you some pointers.

3. *Treat others as you want to be treated (Luke 6:31, Eph 4:32, Eph. 5:21, James 4:11).* There is no question that we humans are messy. We can't have a close relationship without getting hurt. Paul reminded us of this when he said, "Always be humble and gentle. Be patient with each other, making allowance for each other's faults because of your love. Make every effort to keep yourselves united in the Spirit, binding yourselves together with peace" (Eph. 4:2-3, NLT). Sometimes this involves sitting on your hands, zipping your lip, and having a healthy dose of compassion, or skin as thick as an armadillo. There is always a place for gentle one-on-one correction (Matt. 18:15), but this involves a strong transparent friendship that has storm-braving qualities. God promises wisdom if we just ask (James 1:5). A little mercy and grace will go a long way.

4. *True friends make each other better people (1 Thess. 5:11).* Our deepest friendships will be with women who celebrate our successes, cry with us in our heartache, and keep us accountable to move forward with God. Honestly, it's easy to find a group of Christian gals to hang out with and enjoy Bible studies, shopping days, coffee dates, and potluck suppers with. But we all need a couple true friends who will walk with us wherever life's journey takes us.

Jesus had his three: James, John, and Peter. These were men he could bare his soul to. Men who were with him when he sweat drops of blood the night before he was crucified. They were human and fallible. But Jesus loved them in their imperfection.

I call these true friends SIC friends (Sisters in Christ). Our relationships are built foremost on our personal relationships with Jesus and our common spiritual hunger. Looking out for each other, praying with each other, sharing wisdom from the God's word (Col. 3:16), carrying each other's burdens (Gal. 6:2), calling each other out when needed, but always loving with a bond stickier than super glue (Col. 3:14). You need women like this in your life. Find them, cling to them, and never let them go.

We Need a Body

The biblical model of one-anothering contains three types of groups we need to be part of: discipleship groups (SIC friends), small groups (up to twelve or so) and the larger corporate body we worship and learn with.

In Acts 2, we see the model for group fellowship. This corporate body had five earmarks:

1. They devoted themselves to the apostle's teaching and fellowship (v. 42). These early believers all submitted themselves to the teaching of pastors and met regularly with other believers outside church for the breaking of bread.
2. They shared stories of what God was doing in their lives (v. 43). Encouraging one another was part of their regular gathering.
3. They met the needs of all in their group (vv. 44-45). We need to encourage our church bodies to watch over one another and make sure everyone is taken care of physically, mentally, spiritually, and financially.
4. They met together in churches and in homes (v. 46). Hospitality is part of the corporate experience. Be inclusive and welcoming.
5. They experienced growth (v. 47). When we are operating with God's model of corporate fellowship, whether it's small groups or churches, our bodies will grow.

If you are not a part of a corporate body that meets regularly, whether in a house, community building, or church, I encourage you to find one so that you can fulfill the design God has for His people: to gather together to worship Him, to learn from an inspired teacher, and to find fellowship in smaller groups. So many women I know have quit going to church, and it breaks my heart. We need each other. Make a commitment today to start praying for God to lead you to a place where you can serve and be served. There is a body of believers that fits you (Rom. 12:4-8).

My prayer for you: God, help us consider how we may spur one another on toward love and good deeds by meeting together regularly and encouraging one another; singing, listening to your Word, and praying for each other.

DAY ONE: DIGGING DEEPER

Pray and ask God for wisdom as you consider what stood out to you in this week's reading. Write your thoughts in your study journal. Look intently into God's Word, and you will be blessed in what you do (James 1:25).

1. Look up the following one-anothering scriptures and write what each one is asking us to do as part of the body of Christ:
   a. John 13:34-35
   b. Rom. 12:10
   c. 1 Pet. 3:8
   d. 1 Cor. 12:25
   e. Rom. 12:16
   f. 1 Pet. 4:9
   g. Rom. 15:14
   h. James 5:16
   i. 1 Thess. 4:18
   j. Col. 3:16
   k. Heb. 10:24
   l. Gal. 6:2
   m. Eph. 4:2
   n. Eph. 5:21
2. Which "one-anothering" commands are hardest for you and why?

3. Do you have any "iron sharpeners" in your life? How are those friends different from others?

4. Make a list of your closest friends. Are there any on that list that are corrupting your good character or encouraging you to participate in things that take your heart away from God? Pray that God would show you how to put that relationship at a friendly distance so it isn't influential in your life. This will take courage and wisdom.

5. Are you attending a church regularly? If not, why not? Ask God to give you the courage to step out and start hunting for a body of believers you can meet with regularly. Ask your friends where they go to church and consider visiting with them.

6. Do you have a group of SIC friends you are sharing your life with? Ask God to put these women in your life. Keep your eyes and ears open.

7. When you get together with other Christians, do you share stories of what God is doing in your lives? If this is uncomfortable for you, ask God for courage and the right time to start learning how to share these "God sightings" with others. If you're an introvert like me this can be like pulling teeth. I found the book, *The Art of Shouting Quietly,* by Pete Mosley to be a big help.

DAY TWO: LEGACY BUILDING BLOCKS
THE HOSPITALITY CHALLENGE

Truth Fact: A woman finishing well knows that hospitality is about opening our heart and home in Jesus' name to anyone he brings to our door.

In her recent book, *Just Open The Door,* author Jen Schmidt talks about the challenges and rewards of opening your home and your heart to other people. She also challenges the modern definition of hospitality as an entertainment extravaganza and directs our attention to the biblical model of just opening the door. It doesn't matter whether your house is immaculate, your furniture is the latest from Wayfair, or your menu could rival the local five-start bistro. She encourages us to turn away from an event-centered model to a people-centered model.

Practice hospitality as a way of meeting together regularly with people. If the idea of opening your home to people puts a vice grip on your heart and shortens your breath, I'm going to give you some tips to practice pain-free hospitality I've learned from being a confessed introvert. We'll start with events outside your home and work our way to knocking on your door.

1. Invite two or three women to join you at a local coffee shop. This is a pain-free way to start practicing hospitality outside your home.

2. After church, invite someone you know (or another couple, if you are married), out for a quick meal at an inexpensive eatery in the area. If you've already got this habit established, try inviting someone that you just met at the service.

3. If conversation starting is your nemesis, consider buying a set of *Table Topics* cards—they have several different varieties available on Amazon. Also, you can Google "ice breakers" and find lots of helpful suggestions. Keep your crowd in mind when researching topics.

4. Is there a sports event, concert, or play you'd like to attend? Invite several friends to go along and suggest dinner before or coffee after the event. Make the necessary reservations or arrangements for your crowd.

5. If you need moral support to bring a crowd to your own home, enlist a friend who has the gift of hospitality. She can help you figure out what all you need, plan a simple menu, plan who to invite, and even help you serve and host at your place. Don't worry about the house being immaculate. Clean the bathrooms and you're good to go. Remember, it's not the house they're coming to see, it's you.

6. Consider hosting a potluck in your home after church. Make a big pot of chili and ask friends to fill in the gaps. Consider inviting a mixture of people you know and people who are new. Make the food simple and everyone will be at ease. Backs of chips and jars of salsa are always welcome.

DAY THREE: FIRST THINGS FIRST
GATHERING TOGETHER AROUND GOD'S WORD

Since you already have the "Five Ws" for your First Things First morning routine, I want to add another challenge to your spiritual routine: join or host a Bible study. Do you meet together regularly with a small group of women to study the Bible and pray? This kind of study group is a great place to build SIC friends. Studying the Bible in a large auditorium of women is a wonderful experience, but large groups aren't as conducive to building true friendships as home Bible study groups or church-sponsored small groups. If you're not already involved in a small group, let's get you started.

1. Find one or two friends who are interested in joining a small group that meets on a regular basis (I recommend weekly or bi-weekly). Meet together and pray about coming up with a list of women you'd like to invite. When you have ten to twelve names, invite them to join your study. Ask them for days and times that work for them and choose the option that works best for everyone.

2. Next, you'll need to decide what to study. Group members may have recommendations. Get everyone's feedback and choose your curriculum. Who is going to lead? Will you take turns leading? Most curriculums have suggestions for leaders so don't worry about how to lead. Agree on a starting and ending date. You can always keep the group going later but an open calendar will scare some people off.

3. Have some social element incorporated into your schedule so you can have time to build those important individual friendships. My friend and ministry partner, Diane, leads a study group that celebrates monthly birthdays for study members. She plans a party with themes, costumes, and special treats. Consider an outing around a holiday theme or special event you all attend together.

4. Be sure to make prayer a part of your regular study.

5. Honor your friends' time by starting and finishing on time. Refreshments are optional. Talk to your group. I host an evening group of working women that usually bring their own beverages. I have water and decaf available.

6. Consider moving the hosting around to different homes so one person isn't shouldering the whole responsibility.
7. Start organizing this week. Don't put it off. Take the first step.

PART THREE

BUILDING A PERSONAL LEGACY
FIND AND FOLLOW YOUR PURPOSE

"The journey of a thousand miles begins with one step."

—Lao Tzu

"For I know the plans I have for you," declares the Lord, "plans to prosper you and not to harm you, plans to give you hope and a future."

—Jeremiah 29:11

YOU NEED A MAP

My college basketball coach used to say, "nothing happens without a plan." But we all know that stuff happens whether we plan it or not. I like to think that Yogi Berra's accidental wisdom is more to the point when he said, "If you don't know where you are going, you'll end up someplace else." God has paths for us to take, but we need to seek Him to find them. And I'm going to give you a road map to help do just that.

You have spent the last ten chapters training; gathering information, learning new skills and mindsets, digging into God's word, praying, and tracking it all in your journal. Now it's time to step up to the starting line.

In part three, you're going put together a master road map to build a legacy that is uniquely you. We'll take a look at just where God has placed you in life; your values, personality, resources, gifts, strengths, and experiences. We'll look back into your study journal at your circles and communities of influence and chronicle the faces God has placed in your journey. We'll make sure your First Things First routine is suited to your needs and all your legacy building blocks are in place.

The mapping process is exciting—so exciting you may want to rush through it. But stay on your own time schedule. Always keep moving, but don't hurry.

Part three includes extensive online resources in the form of videos, downloadable tools, and resource lists you can access and use to put your map together.

CHAPTER ELEVEN

RECALIBRATING

ON YOUR MARK!

"The LORD says, I will guide you along the best pathway for your life. I will advise you and watch over you."

—Psalm 32:8

On Tuesday, July 30, 2019 I turned twenty-four thousand days old. About fifteen years ago, I started keeping track of my age by days. Inspired by Robert D. Smith's book *20,000 Days and Counting*, I began to look at my life's journey as a daily experience with God. And this particular twenty-four-thousand milestone proved to be a challenge.

My life was turning into one big set of tasks: Finish the book, find a publisher, build a website, transition out of my book marketing business and into ministry, tussle with housing options at our farm, persevere in regaining my health after surgery, and more. I was starting to see my life in terms of performances. Little stage plays, each with several acts of obedience that needed to be presented before an audience of One. Every time I thought I made a mistake in judgment or execution, I got frustrated. Pleasing God was at the top of my list, but I didn't feel very joyful about it.

During my morning quiet time, I began to feel a tug to go back and study John 15. I read through what I had written in chapter 2 of this study. The Holy Spirit began to teach me the difference between performance-related obedience and intentional obedience, or what Jesus called remaining in Him (John 15:9-15). It was like a lazy morning fog was finally giving way to the sunshine.

Setting Your Intention

In John 15:11 Jesus said, "I have told you this so that my joy may be in you and that your joy may be complete." But what had he told us? Remain in His love. And how do we do that? By keeping His commands. But what Jesus is talking about here is not perfection. He's talking about intention. He gave us this command because He knew we could do it, not because he was showing us a gold standard we couldn't possibly reach. He gave us the concept of remaining in Him, so we could have joy. So we could *all* have joy— not just the few super spiritual ones who never make a mistake. And are there really any of those out there anyway? I think I wanted to be one.

Keeping the law (list of dos and don'ts) will not earn us God's love. We already have that. Following Jesus, laying down our life, loving the people God places in our lives, listening for and following where His Spirit leads; that is our "remaining." We need to set our intention on obedience and not focus on our performance as our standard of success. Intention sets our hearts above and sets our hearts free (Ps. 119:32). We need to start from an obedient heart set on commitment, if you will. I would never intentionally choose to fail. I may make the wrong choice in the heat of the moment, but that is not my intent. And this is not easy, but it is the path to finishing well.

Making a New Map

In order to recalibrate our lives to finish well, we need a new map. The old map may have been all about us—mine was. The new map needs to be all about God. Where is He leading you? What does your path to finishing well look like?

Every map has a legend that tells us what the symbols on the map mean. When you're putting together a map to finish well, here are some icons or symbols you may want in your legend:

⚡	Lightning Bolt: God's power in you keeps you remaining in Him (Eph. 3:17-19).
SPEED LIMIT 25	Watch your speed. Be sure to slow down and let God fill you with joy along the way (John 15:11).
⚠️	Caution: Pay attention to your thoughts. Don't be drawn away by the detours (2 Cor. 10:3-5, Phil. 4:8).
🛡️	Armor-Up. Keep the armor of God on at all times (Eph. 6:10-20).
🚫P	No Parking: The world hated Jesus; they will hate us too. This world is not our home (John 15:18-20). Don't get comfortable here.
🤗	Hugs: If we love one another, people will see Jesus in us and be drawn to Him (1 John 4:12).
🕐	Always Keep Praying. Remember your prayer time is not by appointment only; it is perpetual motion.

Creating Your Map

In the next chapter, I'll give you a template to put together your own map to finish well. The information is designed to help you map out your own life's journey, not tell you where to go. I teach you how to collect, analyze, and interpret the information to create your own map. I can't give you my map; you have to create your own. Everyone's map is different.

Your journey to finish well is just beginning. You've got all the right information in this study. Now you just need to set your heart's intention, step up to the starting line with your baton, and run the race God has marked out for you.

Chapter Twelve

TAKING INVENTORY
BUILDING YOUR UNIQUE LEGACY

"Every calling is great when greatly pursued."

—Oliver Wendell Holmes, Jr.

"For we are God's handiwork, created in Christ Jesus to do good works, which God prepared in advance for us to do."

—Ephesians 2:10

Our genetic fingerprint is the DNA that was passed to us from our parents and influenced by our ancestors. According to the National Human Genome Research Institute, 99.9 percent of human DNA is identical from person to person. But in that 0.01 percent, God has formed a human being that is uniquely you.

The first step in building a legacy plan is understanding who God formed you to be. He has made each of us unique:

> For you created my inmost being; you knit me together in my mother's womb. I praise you because I am fearfully and wonderfully made; your works are wonderful, I know that full well.... Your eyes saw my unformed body; all the days ordained for me were written in your book before one of them came to be. (Ps. 139: 13-14, 16).

We will flourish as we embrace that individuality. And we will start our journey of discovery with five truths that lay the foundation of our calling. These are immovable truths about who we are and what God has called us to do.

The Five Truths of Our Calling

God's call to follow Him is unique to each individual. When Jesus called Peter, James, and John, he got their attention by giving them a miraculous catch of fish (Luke 5:4-11). Even though each disciple's call was unique, the purpose of their calling was the same. God equips us to live out our calling with these five truths:

1. *I am created in God's image (Gen. 1:27).* We are created from the same spiritual genetic material as God our Father. And we are His beloved children.
2. *I am unique (Ps. 139:13-14).* God knit you together in your mother's womb. Doesn't that just blow you away? He formed you in the depths of the earth. His eyes saw your unformed body. Every human ever born is his handiwork. And we are all unique.
3. *My divine DNA is housed in a fragile jar of clay (2 Cor. 4:7-9).* That unique spiritual DNA we received by grace is inside an imperfect body that has been limited by sin. Life in the flesh is a constant struggle. But because of God's power in us, we may be struck down, but we will not be destroyed; we are pressed on every side, but we are not crushed. God knows we are weak, but He uses and empowers us anyway.
4. *I am created go do good works (Eph.* 2:10). And it's not up to us to put together that list of good works. God has prepared them in advance for each one of us. We just have to follow His lead.
5. *God has a specific purpose that fits my unique life* (1 Pet. 4:10-11). We have all received gifts from God to serve the people he has put in our lives. God wants us to embrace where he has put us and keep our eyes and ears open for opportunities to administer grace and mercy to those around us.

Taking Inventory

When my husband and I set out to update our housing at the farm we considered many options. Did we want to add on, remodel, get a modular home, or maybe even an adventurous tiny house? But before we could look at any blueprints or make any plans, we needed to consider the layout of the property. Where were all the necessary water and electric connections? And more important, we needed to calculate the actual footprint of the new structure. I quickly realized that taking an inventory of what we had was more important than picking out what we wanted. We had to figure out what would fit not only our needs but our assets.

As our lives change, God's plans for us may look different. Maybe you've been working your whole adult life and now you're not. Maybe you're a full-time caregiver. Maybe you have physical limitations or financial constraints. Maybe your kids are spread out all over the world, or they've just moved back home. Maybe you have just relocated to a new town, or you've been in the same neighborhood your whole life. As Solomon said, "there is a time for everything and a season for every activity under the heavens" (Eccl. 3:1). Wherever you are, God has a plan for you (Jer. 29:11).

What's Next?

There are four steps in the journey to create your unique legacy map. Each step includes exercises to walk through, some questions to answer, and some honest introspection. This whole process can only be defined by one word: Supercalifragilisticexpialidocious. It is magical. You've never experienced anything like the journey you're starting. You're about to find out who you are, where you've been, where you're at now, the people God has put in your life, and how this magical mystery tour will produce your legacy life map.

In the next sections, you'll find out what's involved in putting your legacy map together. If you're ready to build that legacy life, I've put together an online resource that will walk you through all four steps in detail. Why have I put all the important information somewhere else? Because this process is more user-friendly in an online format than in a book. Much of the information you need is housed on the internet and books are not the best medium to use for links and such. Instructions for accessing that inventory resource will be at the end of the chapter. All you need is a phone, a tablet device, or a computer to access the information.

Are you ready to step up to the starting line?

Step One: Know Thyself – Who Am I?

We'll start our journey by taking a series of online assessments that will help you understand your uniqueness—who you were created to be. Links to all the assessments will be in the online bonus material.

We are going to look at five areas that make up your personal profile:

- *Values*: What we feel is important to us and worthy to be pursued. They drive our decisions.
- *Spiritual gifts*: Romans 12:6 says we have different gifts according to the grace we have received.
- *Personality*: We each have a unique outlook, disposition, temperament, and psyche.
- *Strengths:* We all have tasks or actions we do well and that energize us.
- *Passions:* What makes you cry? What makes you angry? What makes you want to take an action? Your passion is closely attached to your emotions.

1. Values

When you start to clarify your values you will be answering questions like:

- Do I want to get involved in volunteer work?
- Do I want to live closer to my family?
- Should I consider a new hobby?

Sometimes looking back helps us clarify our values as well:

- What memories do I have that brought me the most happiness?
- Was there a time in my life I felt more fulfilled? What was I doing?

Our values inform everything we do. They are a foundation for the legacy we are building. My top ten core values are faith, caring, family, compassion, courage, creativity, authority, friendship, loyalty, and generosity. These values inform everything I do.

2. Spiritual Gifts

In 1 Corinthians Paul gives us an explanation of the purpose of spiritual gifts and a list of some of the gifts God has given the church. But the apostle tells us this isn't just a divine grocery list:

There are different kinds of gifts, but the same Spirit distributes them. There are different kinds of service, but the same Lord. There are different kinds of working, but in all of them and in everyone it is the same God at work. Now to each one the manifestation of the Spirit is given for the common good. (1 Cor. 12:4-7)

There are three important truths we need to glean from 1 Corinthians 12:

- God loves diversity (v. 4). There are different kinds of gifts. We don't all serve the body in the same way. I'm thankful for that.
- The gifts are powered by the Holy Spirit (v. 11). I am just the vessel.
- No gift is more important than another. We are to honor all spiritual gifts equally (vv. 15-26).

There are three main lists of spiritual gifts in the New Testament:

- Romans 12: 3-8: Prophecy (speaking out in faith from God's Word), serving others, teaching, encouraging, giving, leadership, showing kindness.
- 1 Corinthians 12: Wisdom, knowledge, faith, healing, miraculous powers, prophecy, discernment, speaking in different languages, interpretation of languages.
- Ephesians 4:7-16: Apostles, prophets, evangelists, pastors, and teacher. These gifts are traditionally designated as gifts specifically given for the church to equip people for works of service.

Knowing your spiritual gifts will help you find opportunities to serve in areas where you'll find the most joy and satisfaction. Knowing how you're gifted can bring a new level of purpose to your relationship with God, a deeper understanding that you are following God's lead. My top three were no surprise: teaching, knowledge, and giving. Teaching, writing, and researching are definitely in my family tree.

3. Personality

Personality can be a misunderstood term. If you look it up in the dictionary you'll find, "the combination of characteristics or qualities that form an individual's distinctive character." I've heard personality described as something you exude, like a perfume. Your personality usually predicts your reactions and informs your interactions.

Knowing your personality profile can give you a better understanding of why you react the way you do, why you approach tasks a certain way, and what your preferences for learning and interacting are. It also helps you understand other people around you. This is what we refer to when we say somebody is wired a certain way. It helps us extend grace and drop our expectations of how people should behave.

4. Passions

Passion is the fuel for action. When you have a passion for something, that energy prompts you to act whether the passion is the result of a positive or negative feeling. You can be passionate about helping abused animals because the idea of abuse breaks your heart or makes you angry. You can be passionate about gardening because being in the dirt gives you a sense of personal peace and you enjoy the resulting beauty. It's important to remember that a passion is usually connected to a strong emotion, which can lead us into trouble if we don't seek God's wisdom about how to activate that passion.

Your passion might be for spending time with family or volunteering wherever your church needs you. There is no one way to live out your passion. But the more we live out our passion, the more engaged we become. How can you discover what you're passionate about if you don't already know? The best way is to answer some questions.

Understanding your passions can help you find opportunities to connect with people who share a like mind. Following our passions will grow our circles of community beyond our faith. It will get us in touch with people who need to see the love of God displayed in someone they share a common ground with.

5. Strengths (Optional)

The Clifton StrengthsFinder assessment was developed by positive psychologist Dr. Donald Clifton. It is a powerful online tool that helps individuals identify and maximize their strengths. Traditional Freudian models of psychology assert that we will have a better life if we tackle what's wrong with us. The StregnthsFinder research asserts people live their best life when they concentrate on their strengths not on their faults.

Understanding your strengths gives you insight into how to be more productive and engaged in whatever you do. Of all the tests mentioned so far, this one has given me the biggest insight into where I can best serve, how I prefer to serve, how I process information and people, and where I'll do best on a team. My top five strengths are Strategic, Significance, Competition, Activator, and Focus.

I list this assessment as an optional assessment because it is not free. If you work or volunteer in any environment where you're on a team, I highly recommend spending the $15 to take the test and get the book.

Step Two: Putting Your Past in Perspective – Where Have I Been?

The Bible is very clear about the role our past should play in our lives. In Philippians 3:13-14 Paul wrote that "forgetting what is behind and straining toward what is ahead. I press on toward the goal to win the prize for which God has called me heavenward in Christ Jesus." The same message is echoed in Colossians 3:5-14 and 2 Corinthians 5:17-19. A close examination of all these verses in context reminds us that our past cannot separate us from God's love. We must rid ourselves of our old selves. Nothing that happened *to us,* or anything *we did* will affect our standing with God.

So why is there a section in this part of the study about using your past to inform your future? Paul was never shy about talking about where he came from. Why is that? Because in his life before Christ, he was a Jew of Jews—a member of the ruling class. His conversion caused quite a stir when he started evangelizing the Gentiles. In the book of Acts, we see that Paul seemed to cause friction wherever he went. And when he finally arrived in Jerusalem, he did not hide. He knew the Jewish rulers were gunning for him. When his bold presence aroused the whole town, Roman guards stepped in and arrested him before the crowd could beat him to death (Acts 21:30-32). Before he was hauled away to jail, he asked for permission to speak to the people.

Paul confidently told the crowd the story of his illustrious past as a persecutor of Christians (Acts 22:1-21). Why? To set the scene for God's call to help establish the new covenant (vs. 6-9). He tells basically the same story in his letter to the Philippians with an exclamation point: "But whatever was to my profit, I now consider loss for the sake of Christ. What is more, I consider everything a loss compared to the surpassing greatness of knowing Christ Jesus my Lord, for whose sake I have lost all things" (Phil. 3:7-11).

Girlfriend, God can use your past to inform your future. Those things we are ashamed of, fearful of recalling, embarrassed of, angry about—those are things God can use to win others. But we must be able to put them in the perspective of our calling. And that sometimes takes some healing. God knows everything about us: every tear we've cried, every time someone took advantage of us or abandoned us, every disappointment, every crushing loss. He's been there with you through it all. And that loss will become your strength, and someone else's comfort and healing (2 Cor. 1:4).

God can use our life experiences: our work experiences, raising our children, caring for aged parents, loss of loved ones, or divorce. Everything positive and negative is part of who we are and what we can do for others. Be thinking of some of the major life events that have shaped who you are. We'll work through some of that in the online assessment at the end of this chapter.

Step Three: Living in the Present – Where Am I Now?

No matter where you want to end up, this is your beginning point. In this section we will examine your current resources: time, finances, physical abilities, and location. Even if you think you are lacking in any of these categories, you are not. God knows where you're at. To Him it's all assets. No judgments assigned. We just need to know what we're working with.

1. Time

We all have twenty-four hours in a day but many of them are already allocated. Do you have a job? Are you a caregiver? Do you have a First Things First morning routine? Do you have regular social engagements? How much time, on average, do you set aside for housekeeping duties, including cleaning and cooking? If you get to the end of this list and have only an hour or two left in your day, this may be your first challenge. We'll address that in the online assessment.

2. Finances and Assets

Sometimes the older we get the less flexible our income becomes. Thankfully, we don't need money to build a legacy life that influences others. Your lack (or abundance) of available money after expenses plays a part in things like how much you can travel, what you can donate or give away, and whether or not you have to continue to work to maintain a status quo.

Your financial assets are also important. You may own a vacation home that could function as a missionary retreat. Owning a car allows you to venture out or give rides to those who don't. You get the idea.

3. Location

All locations are not created equal, but we need to be careful that we don't attach a lack of opportunities to lack of a "meaningful" location. Let me give you a very personal example. In the summer months, I live in just about the most remote place you could think of—a farm in northeast Montana near the Canadian border. The nearest large town is 300 miles away. In the winters, we are fortunate to escape the cold and live in the Phoenix area. Talk about two different ends of the spectrum. Obviously, there are many more opportunities to be involved in all kinds of organizations in an urban area. But here's a truth we need to steep in for a while: Your location is where God has you right now, and He will bring people into your life to influence no matter where you live. It took me many years to appreciate that.

You may or may not live by your children. One of my best friends has all of her nine grandchildren within an hour's drive. In the summer, my nearest child is a day's drive and my nearest grandchild is three day's drive. Even though I am actively involved in building a legacy for them, I cannot see them every day. That distance changes my priorities. That distance is one of the reasons I quit my full-time career. We don't all have that option, so we have to be creative. Building a legacy life is not pain-free. Some of our realities would not be our first choices. But God will use you wherever you are.

Step Four: Who Has God Put in My Life?

In chapter one of our study, you defined your circle of influence and put them on your prayer list. In chapter two, you widened your vision and looked at your communities of influence. In this section we'll get out those lists and take a look at how these people define your map.

Just remember, your family members, children, and grandchildren (if you have them), may not be in your immediate circle of influence. Even though this can feel like a void, even a painful one, it will not stop you from building a legacy life. You are God's handiwork. You were created in Christ Jesus to do the good works He prepared in advance for you to do (Eph. 2:10). And there are plenty of people around you that need you.

On Your Mark

The complete guide to mapping your finishing well journey includes video tutorials, downloadable tools, and more. You can access that process online on the Women Finishing Well website here: https://womenfinishingwell.com/legacy-inventory/

E-mail me at chris@cksyme.com if you have any questions or problems accessing the material.

I also recommend that you join the Facebook study group. There you can connect with women who are on the same journey and get support and encouragement as you navigate your new journey. You can also message me there and ask any questions you have. Here is the link to join: https://www.facebook.com/groups/WomenFinishingWellstudy/

I also cohost a *Women Finishing Well* weekly podcast with my good friend and ministry buddy, Diane Bradley. You can listen and subscribe to our podcast on your podcast app or find it on our website here: https://womenfinishingwell.com/podcast/

Be bold. Be strong. And never, ever quit. I am praying for you to finish well and leave a legacy of faith that lasts for generations.

> "So don't sit around on your hands! No more dragging your feet! Clear the path for long-distance runners so no one will trip and fall, so no one will step in a hole and sprain an ankle. Help each other out. And run for it!"
>
> —Hebrews 12:12-13, The Message

ACKNOWLEDGEMENTS AND THANKS

A writer cannot write a word without the help of many others. Some are there to hold your hand and cheer you on and others are there to help you produce the best possible book you can. These are the people whose names I wish I could put on the front cover.

To my family: You are the reason for this book. Whatever legacy I am leaving—it is for you. I thank God every time I remember you all and always pray for all of you with joy.

To the "Triple "D's": Thanks for being my cheering section. Thanks for reading, praying, sharing, and being the faces I thought of as I wrote this book. You are all building a legacy of faith that will last for generations and much of this book is drawn from your lives.

To my Tuesday-Thursday Bible study ladies: Thanks for bearing with me all the way through this process; for reading and providing valuable feedback and stories that enriched this book. You are all an inspiration.

To my editor, Geoffrey Stone: Your meticulous attention and encouraging thoughts have made this a much better book than it started out. And that's what good editors do!

To Kristen Ingebretson. Thank you creating a beautiful book cover that expresses the essence of my heart about this work.

About The Author

I am a lifelong teacher. I think I was teaching the neighbor kids when I was a toddler. In addition to leading Bible studies, I have taught at the high school, college, and Bible institute levels. My husband would say I am always teaching somebody something. I'm not sure if that's a compliment, but I'll take it.

I am a college sports junkie and had the wonderful experience of working as a media director and marketing person in two different college athletic departments. I've worked many NCAA men's basketball tournament weekends with my younger daughter. It was a blast. #GoZags.

I also had the opportunity to do something many parents dread—work with their children. My oldest daughter is an author and I worked with her as a marketing professional for quite a few years. We sometimes clashed, but always had fun. There is nothing like watching your kids blossom and succeed firsthand. Awesome!

Technically, I have an undergrad degree in English from Montana State (#GoCats) and a graduate degree in Athletics Administration from Eastern Washington University (#GoEags) where I did my thesis work in crisis management (how appropriate to my life). I also earned a certificate in Pastoral Leadership from the Yellowstone Valley Bible Institute in Billings, Montana (there is no hashtag for that school's mascot). Can I add antiques dealer and caterer to this list? It's making me tired just writing all this. I am living a full life and have been blessed. My husband and I farm in northeast Montana near the Canadian border and escape the cold winters in the Phoenix area. God is good.

I love to speak at women's events and you can get information about that here: https://womenfinishingwell.com/speaking/

God bless you, my friends.

-Chris